STAFFORDSHIRE LIBRARY AND INFORMATION SERVICES

LS Please return or renew by the last date shown

If not required by other readers, this item may be renewed
in person, by post or telephone, online or by email.
To renew, either the book or ticket are required.

24 HOUR RENEWAL LINE - 0845 33 00 740

CLASSIC BIOGRAPHIES
EDITED BY RICHARD HOLMES

Defoe on Sheppard and Wild
Johnson on Savage
Godwin on Wollstonecraft
Southey on Nelson
Gilchrist on Blake
Scott on Zélide

JOHNSON ON SAVAGE

An Account of the Life of Mr. Richard Savage, Son of the Earl Rivers

by
Samuel Johnson, LL.D

With three essays on Biography

EDITED WITH AN INTRODUCTION BY
RICHARD HOLMES

HARPER PERENNIAL
London, New York, Toronto and Sydney

Harper Perennial
An imprint of HarperCollins*Publishers*
77–85 Fulham Palace Road,
Hammersmith, London w6 8jb

www.harperpernnial.co.uk

This Harper Perennial published 2005
1

The Life of Mr. Richard Savage first published 1744

Introduction Copyright © Richard Holmes 2005

A catalogue record for this book
is available from the British Library

ISBN 0-00-711169-X

Set in PostScript Linotype Adobe Caslon
and Spectrum Display by
Rowland Phototypesetting Ltd,
Bury St Edmunds, Suffolk

Printed and bound in Great Britain by
Clays Ltd, St Ives plc

CONTENTS

INTRODUCTION

1

'A shilling life will give you all the facts,' wrote W.H. Auden in his wry sonnet about the shortcomings of biography. But very few facts are known with absolute certainty about the flamboyant 18th century poet who called himself Richard Savage (including his real identity). Yet he is the subject of one of the greatest short biographies in the English language.

One fact is that Savage always claimed to be 'son of the late Earl Rivers', but could never prove it. Another is that he was convicted of killing a man in a brothel near Charing Cross, London, on 20 November 1727. A third is that he published a bestselling poem called 'The Bastard' in 1728, which ran to five editions in five months. A fourth is that he died penniless in a debtors' prison in Bristol in 1743. To which we can add a fifth, that his *Life* was written by Samuel Johnson.

In January 1744, the *London Evening Post* carried the following tantalizing advertisement for this biography.

> An account of the life of Mr Richard Savage, son of the late Earl Rivers. Who was, soon after he came into the world, bastardised by an act of Parliament; and deprived of the title and estate to which he was born; was committed by his mother, the Countess of Macclesfield, to a poor woman, to be bred up as her own son; came to the knowledge of his real mother, now alive, but abandoned by her, persecuted, and condemned for

murder, and against all her endeavours, pardoned; made Poet Laureate to Queen Caroline, became very eminent for his writings, of which many are quoted in this Work, particularly 'The Bastard' and the *Wanderer* . . . went into Wales, to be supported by a subscription, promoted by Mr Pope, but at last died in Prison.

Johnson's unlikely friendship with Savage, which inspired this extraordinary work, is one of the strangest episodes in Johnson's whole career. It belongs to his earliest and darkest days in London, long before he had published his great *Dictionary* (1755), or formed his Club, or met his own biographer James Boswell (1763). Sir John Hawkins, one of the very few people who knew both Johnson and Savage at this obscure time, remarked that it was 'an intimacy, the motives for which may probably seem harder to account for, than any one particular in his entire life'.

Boswell later agreed with this uneasy verdict: 'Richard Savage: a man of whom it is difficult to speak impartially, without wondering that he was for some time the intimate companion of Johnson; for his character was marked by profligacy, insolence and ingratitude.' He added that Savage had a reputation for 'fire, rudeness, pride, meanness, and ferocity'.

But he may also have appeared a curiously glamorous figure to Johnson. At the time they first met in 1737, 'Sam' Johnson was not the great Doctor of later legend. He was 29 years old, an aspiring but virtually unpublished author from the provinces. Large, shambling, grotesquely scarred by childhood scrofula, he was subject to physical convulsions and disabling episodes of mental depression. Abrupt and awkward in company, he was a unsuccessful schoolmaster from Lichfield, who had come up to London (with his last pupil David Garrick) to try his literary fortunes by contributing poems and translations to the *Gentleman's Magazine.*

By contrast, Richard Savage, then in his early forties (his exact birthdate is uncertain), was a stylish, celebrated and even notorious personality in literary London. Universally known in the coffee-houses, he cut a dandyish figure as observed by Hawkins. 'Savage, as to his exterior, was to a remarkable degree, accomplished; he was a handsome, well-made man, and very courteous in the modes of salutation'. Hawkins added dryly: 'I have been told that in taking off his hat and disposing it under his arm, and in his bow, he displayed as much grace as those actions were capable of.'

For most of his life Savage had claimed to be the illegitimate offspring of a love-affair between the Countess Macclesfield and Richard Savage, the 4th Earl Rivers. This claim had never been recognised, and remains unproven to this day. But Lord Rivers having died in 1712, Savage had begun to style himself 'natural Son of the Late Earl Rivers', and for more than twenty years pursued his claims against the wealthy, widowed Lady Macclesfield, with heroic – or relentless – determination. This became the subject of his notorious poem 'The Bastard', published in 1728, shortly after he had received the royal pardon for the murder at Charing Cross:

> Blest be the *Bastard's* birth! Through wond'rous ways
> He shines eccentric like a Comet's blaze.
> No sickly fruit of faint compliance he;
> He! Stampt in nature's mint of extasy!
> He lives to build, not boast, a gen'rous race:
> No tenth transmitter of a foolish face.

This brisk, ebullient declaration still enshrines Savage in the modern *Oxford Dictionary of Quotations.* Less well-known is the

subsequent passage in which he sardonically and publicly thanks
Lady Macclesfield for his illegitimacy:

> O Mother, yet *no* Mother – 'tis to you,
> My thanks for such distinguish'd claims are due.
> You, unenslav'd to Nature's narrow laws,
> Warm championess for *Freedom's* sacred cause,
> From all the dry devoirs of blood and line,
> From ties maternal, moral and divine,
> Discharg'd my grasping soul; push'd me from shore,
> And launch'd me into life without an oar.

Although Savage's campaigns and publications between 1724 and
1737 sometimes have the appearance of blackmail, young Johnson
was profoundly touched by his oft-repeated tale of emotional
rejection and maternal persecution. Though since the real Lady
Macclesfield was still alive and living in Old Bond Street,
London, it is perhaps curious that Johnson neither attempted
to interview her nor correspond with her. Nevertheless, the motif
of Savage's 'cruel Mother' drives the early part of his biography
with vivid conviction, summoning a kind of fairy-tale power and
imagery.

> Such was the beginning of the life of Richard Savage. Born with
> a legal claim to honour and to affluence, he was, in two months,
> illegitimated by the Parliament, and disowned by his mother,
> doomed to poverty and obscurity, and launched upon the ocean
> of life, only that he might be swallowed by its quicksands, or
> dashed upon its rocks. (p.6)

Johnson was not the only one to be so moved. Savage was also
known as one of the most shameless and successful financial
spongers in London. With his poignant story of the 'cruel
Mother' he had at various times succeeded in obtaining money
from the essayist Sir Richard Steele, the actress Anne Oldfield,

the editor Aaron Hill, the Irish peer and literary patron Lord Tyrconnel (Lady Macclesfield's nephew), and none other than the great poet Alexander Pope, who eventually organized a charitable subscription for Savage's benefit in 1739.

All these episodes are recounted with shrewd insight by Johnson in the *Life*, including the 'mournful' fact that they nearly all ended in furious quarrels. 'It was his peculiar happiness that he scarcely ever found a stranger whom he did not leave a friend; but it must likewise be added that he had not often a friend long, without obliging him to become a stranger. (p. 41)

Possibly his most astonishing financial coup was the grant of a royal pension by the Queen. Savage had unsuccessfully applied for the post of Poet Laureate to the new King George II in 1731 (just 4 years after his trial for murder). Having been rejected in favour of Colley Cibber, he had unblushingly appointed himself 'Volunteer Laureate to Queen Caroline', and begun publishing an annual Birthday Ode in her honour, for which he was paid a pension of £50 a year, until the Queen's death in 1737. Johnson records this 'odd' triumph, together with Cibber's acid observation that Savage might with 'equal propriety style himself a Volunteer Lord or Volunteer Baronet'. (p.56)

This did not prevent Savage from eventually descending into absolute poverty in London. Significantly perhaps, this was at the very time he first met Johnson, so that the shared nightmare experience of indigence in Grub Street, without proper food or lodgings, became another powerful bond between the two men. It is an experience that also shapes the second half of the biography, and its most dramatic passages of appeal to the reader's sympathy.

This was also the first time that young Johnson was temporarily separated from his wife Tetty (who remained back in

Lichfield), and was exposed to all the temptations and seductions of the capital city. Boswell recalls that at the very end of his life, Johnson looked back at it with uneasiness and perhaps, also, some secret nostalgia. 'His conduct, after he came to London, and had associated with Savage and others, was not so strictly virtuous, in one respect, as when he was a younger man [at Lichfield]. It was well known that his amorous inclinations were uncommonly strong and impetuous ... in his combats with them, he was sometimes overcome.'

2

Johnson heard of Savage's death in Bristol in August 1743, through their mutual friend Edward Cave, the editor of the *Gentleman's Magazine*. It was evidently a great personal blow to him, as he immediately determined to write Savage's Life. Johnson had in fact already published several short biographical essays with Cave, notably on the piratical sailor Sir Francis Drake (1740), and the Dutch scientist Herman Boerhaave (1739). But this was to be his first attempt at a full length biography on a contemporary subject from original materials. It was also the first to be written *con amore*. It would eventually run to a book of 180 pages (45,000 words), much longer than any of his subsequent *Lives of the Poets*.

Within three weeks he announced his intention to defend 'the unfortunate and ingenious Mr Savage', in a long letter to the magazine that Cave published in September. The Life would 'speedily be published by a person who was favoured with his Confidences, and received from himself an Account of most of his Transactions'. This Life would be authentic, and would preserve Savage's memory from 'insults and calumnies'. Johnson then made an historic and combative claim about the nature of biography, distinguishing it from romance or fiction.

> It may be reasonably imagined that others may have the same Design, but as it is not credible that they can obtain the same Materials, it must be expected they will supply from Invention the want of Intelligence, and that under the Title of the *Life of Savage* they will publish only a Novel filled with romantick Adventures, and imaginary Amours. You may therefore perhaps gratify the Lovers of Truth and Wit by giving me leave to inform them in your Magazine, that my Account will be published in 8vo by Mr Roberts of Warwick-Lane.

Johnson had several different kinds of material to draw on. For a start, he had talked a great deal with Savage, and heard his story at length from his own mouth. The accounts of Johnson and Savage walking and talking together all night through the London streets in 1737–8, especially around Westminster and St James's Square, were eventually to became legendary. This is how Sir John Hawkins remembered them:

> Johnson has told me, that whole nights have been spent by him and Savage in conversation of this kind, not under the hospitable roof of a tavern, where warmth might have invigorated their spirits, and wine dispelled their care; but in a perambulation round the squares of Westminster, St James's in particular, when all the money the could raise was less than sufficient to purchase them the shelter and sordid comforts of a night cellar . . .

A later friend and biographer, the Irish poet Arthur Murphy, gently embroidered on Johnson's memories, and moving their location slightly westwards into fashionable Mayfair, gave them an exquisite touch of Dublin absurdity. 'Johnson has been often heard to relate, that he and Savage walked round Grosvenor

Square till four in the morning; in the course of their conversation reforming the world, dethroning princes, establishing new forms of government, and giving laws to the several states of Europe, till fatigued at length with their legislative office, they began to feel the want of refreshment; but could not muster up more than fourpence halfpenny.'

It is therefore particularly interesting that Johnson chooses never to introduce himself explicitly into the *Life of Savage*. This reticence is unlike, for example, Boswell who appears in *propria persona* throughout his *Life of Johnson* (1791); or William Godwin who plays a decisive role in the second half of his *Memoirs* (1798) of Mary Wollstonecraft. Johnson makes only one passing reference to himself in the third person, at the fateful moment in 1739, when Savage finally leaves London for Wales, never to return. Yet this moment is intensely emotional.

'Full of these salutary resolutions, [Savage] left London in July 1739, having taken leave, with great tenderness, of his friends, and parted with the author of this narrative with tears in his eyes'. (p.85). Johnson's sentence seems to leave deliberately ambiguous whether the tears belonged to himself or Savage. Perhaps this was deliberate. But in a marginal note later added to a copy he was correcting in 1748, Johnson wrote: 'I had then a slight fever'. This surely claims the tears – and the intense emotion – as his own.

Johnson's personal identification with Savage's fate is one of the most subtle issues underlying the entire biography. It deeply affects his partial handling of evidence, and wonderfully colours the continuous, shifting ambiguity of its narrative tone. Young Johnson makes common cause with Savage, in his bohemian style of life, his love of late-night talk, his proud sense of being a social outcast, and in his intense political anger at oppression by the rich and powerful. Yet this same self-identification produces strange biographical distortions. How deeply Johnson's feelings were engaged, and how far objective biography becomes distilled into subjective autobiography, is one of the enduring mysteries of its power, and raises larger questions about the whole genre.

3

Johnson took about 3 months compiling and expanding the biography, between mid-September and 14 December 1743, when he signed a receipt for 15 guineas on delivery of the manuscript to Cave. In January 1744, in a deadline crisis familiar to many biographers, he 'sat up all night' correcting and revising the last 'forty-eight pages of the printed octavo', probably because he had just received copies of Savage's last three letters from Bristol. The *Life* was finally published in February 1744.

During this time he sent several notes to his editor, many of them giving painful glimpses of the Grub Street writer's life which he had shared with Savage. Once, the printer's boy finds Johnson 'writing this, almost in the dark' because he lacks candles. Later he is writing hard but lacks 'good Pens'. Then he has been ill, the writing has been interrupted, but he is 'almost well again' and so humbly begs 'another Guinea' in advance. Finally, most bleakly of all, he is *'impransus'* – supperless. Meanwhile he bombards Cave with requests for further information. 'Towards Mr Savage's Life what more have you got?' He asks for a transcript of Savage's trial for murder; for a copy of his Defence speech at the Old Bailey; and a copy of his 1726 *Miscellaneous Poems*, 'on account of the Preface' which attacks Lady Macclesfield. He also wants some articles in the *Plain Dealer*

describing Savage's case, and 'all the Magazines that have anything of his or relating to him'.

Johnson had all Savage's major publications to draw on, and
several of his rare letters (less than 30 are known) preserved by
Cave at the *Gentleman's Magazine*, especially those Savage had
written from Newgate Gaol in Bristol in 1743. Johnson would
use extracts from these to powerful effect in the final section of
the Life, showing the extraordinary shifts in pose and self-
presentation which Savage was capable of adopting. Even when
cornered and reduced to the most desperate circumstances,
Savage was incorrigeable and changeling-like.

He also had copies of the poems and essays that Aaron Hill had
published during the *Plain Dealer's* campaign of 1724 to establish
Savage's claim against Lady Macclesfield. Most remarkable
among these was Savage's 'Lament', published in June 1724. In it
Savage transforms his 'cruel Mother' into a cruel Lover.

> Hopeless, abandoned, aimless, and oppress'd,
> Lost to Delight, and every Way distress'd;
> Cross his cold Bed, in wild Disorder thrown,
> Thus sigh'd Alexis, friendless and alone -
> 'Why do I breathe? - What joy can Being give?
> When she, who gave me Life, forgets I live!
> Feels not these wintry blasts; - nor heeds my Smart;
> But shuts me from the Shelter of her Heart! . . .

In the first edition of the Life, Johnson printed extensive extracts
from these works in a score of footnotes, many of them several
pages long, which almost amounted to a separate anthology.
Besides the 'Lament', he drew notably on the libelous (and
hastily suppressed) 'Preface to the *Miscellaneous Poems*' of 1726,
'The Bastard', *The Wanderer*, 'The Volunteer Laureates', and
'London and Bristol Delineated'. Though fascinating, they

obstruct the natural flow of the biographical narrative, and he eventually omitted them in definitive edition incorporated into the *Lives of the Eminent English Poets* in 1781.

4

Johnson had one other major biographical source of information. He obtained from Cave a 29 page pamphlet written anonymously at the time of Savage's conviction for murder in 1727. It was entitled *The Life of Mr Richard Savage . . . Who was Condemned at the last Sessions of the Old Bailey, for Murder . . . With some very remarkable Circumstances relating to the Birth and Education of that Gentleman, which were Never before made Publick.* This was the pamphlet, hurriedly organized by Aaron Hill, intended to save Savage from the hangman's noose. It was dashed off in 2 days by a fellow Grub Street journalist, one Thomas Cooke, who worked in the upstairs room of a Fleet Street tavern, hoping to save '*a brother poet* – how unworthy soever of the appellation' from the gallows. It was from this work that Johnson drew his extraordinary portrait of Lady Macclesfield, which dramatically sets the combative tone of the opening.

Johnson's righteous anger is felt throughout this early section, with an unrelenting series of attacks on Lady Macclesfield's 'barbarous', 'cruel' and 'unnatural' behaviour. He recounts a breathless (and gripping) series of incidents in which she denies Savage's birthright, suppresses his name, farms him out to a nurse, frustrates a £300 inheritance, attempts to apprentice him to a shoemaker, and dispatch him to the American colonies. Finally she promotes his execution by seeking to prevent the royal pardon. (p.26–7)

The mounting bitterness of these accusations, their rhetorical force, and their melodramatic repetitions, cannot quite hide from an alert reader their curious and unsubstantiated nature. Most problematic of all, Johnson can find no real motive – moral, prudential or pecuniary – for these maternal crimes. (p.5). Yet it is difficult to doubt Johnson's good faith, and since Lady Macclesfield was still alive (a point he reiterates), one assumes he had documentary evidence that would have protected him and his publisher against libel.

But he did not. All these stories were simply taken from the *Old Bailey* pamphlet of 1727. No doubt they were confirmed by Savage in his long conversations with Johnson, yet the fact is that they have no other independent documentary source. Even the 'convincing Original Letters' which Savage claimed he had discovered and proved his birth, were never actually produced. They are mentioned in the *Old Bailey* pamphlet, and the editor Aaron Hill claimed he once saw them in 1724, but they were never printed and have long since disappeared. One concludes that Johnson simply wanted – *or needed* – to believe Savage's version of events. And to defend Savage, he must also make his reader believe.

Johnson's defence of Savage's whole disastrous life – the sponging, the blackmail, the murder charge, the ingratitude to his patron Tyrconnel; and later the obscene poetry, the reckless improvidence, the moral blindness, and the self-destructive behaviour in London and Bristol – depends upon his convincing the reader that Savage was a lifelong victim of Lady Macclesfield's persecutions. So she is consistently presented as Savage's evil star, his nemesis, his avenging angel.

> This mother is still alive, and may, perhaps, even yet, though her malice was so often defeated, enjoy the pleasure of reflecting

that the life which she often endeavored to destroy, was at least shortened by her maternal offices; that, though she could not transport her son to the plantations, bury him in the shop of a mechanick, or hasten the hand of the public executioner, she has yet had the satisfaction of embittering all his hours, and forcing him into exigencies that hurried his death. (p.28)

Over forty years later, Boswell the professional biographer and trained lawyer (he had a brilliant success in defending a sheep-stealer at the Scottish Bar) was also strangely puzzled by what he saw as Johnson's credulousness over Savage's claims. 'Johnson's partiality for Savage made him entertain no doubt of his story, however extraordinary and improbable. It never occurred to him to question his being the son of the Countess of Macclesfield, of whose unrelenting barbarity he so loudly complained, and the particulars of which are related in so strong and affecting a manner in Johnson's Life of him.'

His own subsequent researches cast much doubt over the entire story and left him, in a memorable phrase, 'vibrating in uncertainty'. Modern scholars, like Clarence Tracy and James L. Clifford, have felt the same perplexity. (See Further Reading)

It is interesting that the great French Enlightenment critic and novelist Denis Diderot, in a review of a French translation of the *Life* which appeared in Paris in 1771, also singled out the peculiar nature of Johnson's handling of Lady Macclesfield. He wondered, with a wry smile, if a fiction-writer would have got away with it. 'This Countess of Macclesfield is a strange woman, persecuting a love-child with a rage sustained for many years, never extinguished and founded on nothing. If a writer decided to introduce, in a play or a novel, a character of this kind, it would be booed.' The implication is that Johnson has broken the Aristotelian rule of 'probability'.

Yet Diderot finally gives Johnson (not after all a French classi-
cist) the benefit of the doubt. 'Nevertheless it is compatible
with reality. And is reality then sometimes to be booed? Why
not! Does it never deserve it?' It has been suggested that the
chameleon anti-hero of Diderot's own subsequent novel, *Le
Neveu de Rameau*, may partly have been inspired by Savage's
machinations.

It is certainly possible that Savage may have been what he
constantly, obsessively, unfailingly (even under sentence of
death) claimed to be: Lady Macclesfield rejected son. Johnson
may have been right: his honesty and intellectual judgement
were always formidable After all, he later saw through the claims
of the epic poet 'Ossian', and the Rowley 'forgeries' of Thomas
Chatterton. On the other hand, his profound sympathy for
Savage may simply have misled him. His later confidante, Hester
Thrale remarked tenderly: 'Dear Dr Johnson was not difficult
to be imposed on where the *Heart* came into question.'

Yet there is a strange fury in these biting, unsubstantiated
denunciations of Lady Macclesfield which suggest other,
obscurer forces at work. They might perhaps be connected with
young Johnson's own darker feelings towards women: his repul-
sive appearance, his difficulties with his wife Tetty (20 years
his senior and increasingly reliant on 'cordials'); and his own
unloving mother Sarah Johnson.

A modern poet and biographer, John Wain, has speculated
in this direction rather further than Boswell. 'There were also
deeper emotional reasons. Savage had, by his own account, been
cruelly rejected by an unnatural mother. Now Johnson, as we
have seen, had strong and ambivalent feelings towards his own
mother . . . This resentment of Sarah for her failure to give him
love and emotional security was buttoned down tightly out of

sight and watched over by an unsleeping censor. All the more eagerly did he listen to Savage's tirades against the mother who had similarly, and far more spectacularly, failed him. Chords which his own fingers were forbidden to touch became vibrant at the eloquent recital of Savage's wrongs. How deep did Savage's influence go? Very deep, I think. His presence touched the hidden springs of Johnson's deep feelings, and may, here and there, have caused some strange streams to gush from the rock. He was, for some crucial months, closer to Johnson than anyone else. Certainly, closer than Tetty.' (Wain, 1974)

5

Yet there is a further layer to the enigma. An attentive reading of the *Old Bailey* pamphlet, which was after all written specifically to exculpate Savage, also suggests that Johnson – out of loyalty – may have been avoiding a much harsher possible interpretation of Savage's character in the early years. Leaving aside the historical truth of Savage's claims, one begins to ask *just who was persecuting whom*?

Savage's emotional appeals to Lady Macclesfield as the hopeless, abandoned, sighing 'Alexis' in 1724, have within three years later taken on a far more aggressive and imperious tone. With the publication of his *Miscellaneous Poems* of 1726, shortly before the unfortunate murder, he seems to be conducting something indistinguishable from a successful blackmail campaign. How else should one interpret the following passage from *Old Bailey*?

> He had also wrote a long Preface to [the Poems], giving some Account of his Mother's unparalleled ill Treatment of him; but was prevail'd on through the imposition of some very

considerable Persons to cancel it; and about that time he had a Pension of 50 pounds a year settled upon him. It will not venture to say whether this Allowance came from *her*, or, if so, upon what Motives she was induced to grant it; but choose to leave the Reader to guess at it.

Johnson also avoids the notion of blackmail in his account of the subsequent publication of Savage's most famous poem, 'The Bastard'.

It was the most severe and successful attack Savage had ever mounted against Lady Macclesfield, and her public humiliation at Bath is fully, and indeed appreciatively described by Johnson, as an act of necessary justice for a lifetime's persecution. He accordingly assigns its publication to 1735, after Lord Tyrconnel had withdrawn his splendid £200 annual pension, and Savage was once again reduced to poverty. (See Select Chronology.) The poem is presented as Savage's final, bitter and fully justified riposte. 'Thus Savage had the satisfaction of finding that, though he could not reform his mother, he could punish her, and that he did not always suffer alone.' (p.50)

But either deliberately, or unconsciously, Johnson has crucially altered the publication date to suit his defence of Savage. The fact – one of those few, definite 'shilling' facts – is that 'The Bastard', in all 5 of its editions, appeared seven years earlier in the spring and summer of 1728. It appeared, therefore, shortly *before* Lady Macclesfield's nephew Lord Tyrconnel made Savage the £200 pension, and therefore seems to have had an entirely different motivation. It may certainly be seen as a successful demand for money, with menaces. £200 per annum was the cost of silence, and it is true that Savage published nothing again against Lady Macclesfield until the pension was abruptly terminated (after a quarrel) in 1735.

The *Old Bailey* pamphlet also first mentions the romantic 'candle' incident, which so moved Johnson and seems to summon up a whole world of tragic outcasts, rejected children, and homeless wanderers. This is the emotive picture his source draws.

> While Nature acted so weakly on the Humanity of the Parent, she seems on the Son's side to have doubled her usual Influence. Even the most shocking personal Repulses, and a severity of Contempt and Injuries received at her Hands, through the whole Course of his Life, were not able to erase from his Heart the impressions of his filial Duty; nor, which is more strange, of his Affection. I have known him walk three or four Times in a dark Evening, through the Street this Mother lives in, only for the melancholy Pleasure of looking up at her Windows, in hopes to catch a Moment's Sight of her as she might cross the Room by Candlelight.

Johnson brilliantly deploys and develops this memorable image of the outcast in the dark streets, adding layers of pathos and irony. 'But all his assiduity and tenderness were without effect, for he could neither soften her heart nor open her hand, and was reduced to the utmost miseries of want, while he was endeavoring to awaken the affection of a mother. He was therefore, obliged to seek some other means of support, and having no profession, became by necessity an author.' (p.9–10)

But in order to sustain the pathetic, benighted picture of young Savage, Johnson is compelled to hold over in the chronology of his narrative the alarming 'stalking' incident in which these evening vigils culminated. This incident is 'omitted in the order of time' (as he cautiously explains) until it can be more safely placed in the account of Savage's trial. So only when Savage is himself in danger of death, does Johnson reveal the supremely damaging story of Savage actually slipping into Lady

Macclesfield's Old Bond Street house at night, silently entering her bedroom, and only thinking it 'prudent to retire' when the terrified woman , fearful of 'murder', woke the whole household with her 'screams'. This was, Johnson calmly asserts, nothing but 'a fictitious assault'. (p.26)

Indeed Johnson's handling of the entire trial is a masterpiece of forensic legerdemain, in which he appears to be adopting a cool and judicious stance, while actually arguing passionately for the defence. A transcript of the actual trial has survived (see Further Reading), and it reveals how brilliantly Johnson deflected the hostile evidence of the landlady and her maid; ignored the deposition of the surgeon (who demonstrated how Savage's fatal sword-thrust could not have been delivered when the murdered man Sinclair was in 'a posture of defence'); and played the distracting card of Lady Macclesfield's vindictiveness. In his ringing phrase, 'Thus had Savage perished by the evidence of a bawd, a strumpet, and his mother . . .' (p.27).

Johnson's triumph is the handling of the condemnation speech of the Judge, Mr Justice Page. Francis Page was a notorious 'hanging judge' (also caricatured by Henry Field in *Tom Jones*, 1749), and on the West Country circuit there was a popular song, 'God in his rage made old Judge Page'. But no authentic record exists of his summing-up in this case. Johnson simply invents it. For this Johnson could claim the classical authority of Tacitus, who invents the speeches of his heroes at signal moments. But he does better than this, by claiming that this 'eloquent harangue' is exactly 'as Mr Savage used to relate it'. (p.24). He transforms Judge Page's judgement into an theatrical comedy, as Savage afterwards used to perform it for admiring friends. The judge's grim appeals to the 'Gentleman of the Jury', are farcically turned to Savage's advantage.

6

Up to this point in the biography, Johnson appears largely in the role of Savage's advocate, skillfully pleading his case, plangently emphasising his misfortunes, and thunderously attacking his enemies. It is a brilliant rhetorical performance. The reader is wonderfully gripped and impressed, even if not entirely convinced. But from the moment Savage is pardoned in 1728, and his fashionable 'golden' period of social success and patronage begins, a subtle change starts to steal over Johnson's narrative. (p.32)

Melodrama shifts to satire, increasingly at Savage's expense. A note of black comedy creeps in, and Savage's outrageous behaviour towards Lord Tyrconnel points towards something incorrigeable and profoundly damaged in his nature. He luxuriates in the wealthy patronage, but also exploits it shamelessly and thoughtlessly. He causes chaos in Lord Tyrconnel's apartments; he orders about his servants; he brings cronies back to the house late at night, and drinks his cellars dry of their best wines. 'Having given him a collection of valuable books, stamped with his own arms, [Tyrconnel] had the mortification to see them, in a short time, exposed to sale upon the stalls, it being usual with Mr Savage, when he wanted a small sum, to take his books to the pawnbroker.' (p.41)

As Savage repeatedly fails to take control of his life, there is a new note of philosophical reflection. Imperceptibly, advocacy gives way to moral enquiry. Savage's character, rather than his brazen claims, gradually becomes Johnson's central concern, and he sees him embarked on a never-ending Dantesque treadmill of self-deception. 'He proceeded throughout his life to tread the

same steps on the same circle; always applauding his past conduct, or at least forgetting it to amuse himself with phantoms
of happiness, which were dancing before him; and willingly
turned his eyes from the light of reason, when it would have
discovered the illusion, and shown him, what he never wished
to see, his real state.' (p.52)

The episodes of the Volunteer Laureateship, the publication
of the obscene poem 'The Progress of a Divine', and the disastrous quarrel with Tyrconnel mark a steadily downward trajec-
tory. Now black comedy is shifting towards a more human and
universal tragedy. Johnson himself seems to move closer to the
narrative surface. We become increasingly aware, if only sublim-
inally, of Johnson as the shrewd eyewitness. He is the sympath-
etic companion, but the also undeceived judge of character

Observing Savage's mixture of professional pride and childlike
vanity as a poet, he recalls with a painful smile. 'He could not
easily leave off, once he had begun to mention himself and his
works; nor ever read his verses without stealing his eyes from
the page, to discover in the faces of his audience, how they were
effected by any favourite passage.' (p.103) Such a remark could
only have been made by someone who had spent, and perhaps
endured, many hours in Savage's company.

Johnson's presence as the anonymous observer, or unnamed
'friend' increases throughout the penultimate part of the biography that covers Savage's return, in the winter of 1737–8, to
the lonely and humiliating poverty of Grub Street (p.70).

Many incidents begin to reflect Johnson's own experiences at
Lichfield and Oxford, such as the shameful time well-meaning
friends left him a pair of boots at his college door when he was a
poverty-stricken undergraduate. Savage's friends also humiliated
him with good intentions. Savage 'came to the lodgings of a

friend [clearly Johnson] with the most violent agonies of rage; and, being asked what it could be that gave him such disturbance, he replied, with the utmost vehemence of indignation, 'that they had sent for a tailor to measure him.' (p.83)

Savage's love of conversation, his hunger for company, and terror of loneliness are also, hauntingly, those of the isolated and depressive young Johnson. 'He was generally censured for not knowing when to retire; but that was not the defect of his judgement, but of his fortune: when he left his company, he was frequently to spend the remaining part of the night in the street, or at least abandoned to gloomy reflections, which is not strange that he delayed as long as he could; and sometimes forgot that he gave others pain to avoid it himself.' (p.102)

This whole section is dominated by the bleak image of the night-walks which they shared for several months in 1738–9. Here Johnson's great elegiac summary of Savage's harsh misfortunes and missed opportunities, is written in a tragic register that is quite unlike anything that has proceeded it. 'On a bulk, in a cellar, or in a glass-house, among thieves and beggars, was to be found the author of the *Wanderer*; the man of exalted sentiments, extensive views, and curious observations; the man whose remarks on life might have assisted the statesman, whose ideas of virtue might have enlightened the moralist, whose eloquence might have influenced senates, and whose delicacy might have polished courts.'(p.70)

Johnson is also more and more present in the precision, deliberation and authority of his style. In a favoured rhetorical device (technically known as *ironic chiasmus*, or reversal of terms) he repeatedly gives Savage generous praise with one hand, only to withdraw it regretfully with the other. 'He was remarkably retentive of his ideas, which, when once he was in possession of them, rarely forsook him; a quality which could never be communicated to his money.' (p.74) This gesture of reversed and suspended judgement, like a musical motif, begins to dominate the entire biographical composition. The delicate, almost trembling fluctuation between praise and condemnation, love and mockery, sympathy and reproach, becomes a central truth of the *Life*. It also expresses Johnson's generous, but essentially tragic view of human nature.

7

In the final section of the biography, Johnson makes a last brilliant adjustment to the tone and angle of his narrative. It is clear that he disapproves of Savage's delusory scheme to 'retire' into rural Wales, and live off the subscription organized by Pope, until he has re-written his failed play *Sir Thomas Overbury*. But his account is subtly and sympathetically pitched. It begins in a gentle satire of Savage's dreamlike ideas of country life, 'of which he had no knowledge but from pastorals and songs', and where he fondly imagined that 'the melody of the nightingale' was to be heard 'from every bramble'. This seems unavoidably like the echo of an actual conversation they had. (p.82) But it ends in the bleak reporting of a nightmare, with Savage ill, penniless and friendless in Bristol, sleeping in the garret of an 'obscure inn' by day (probably drunk); and slipping out by night – again that theme of obsessive night-walking – only to avoid creditors and restore 'the action of his stomach by a cordial.' (p.90).

Yet once in the debtor's prison, Johnson tenderly shows many of Savage's strongest qualities reasserting themselves: his wit, his stoicism, his inexhaustible interest in those around him (even the lowest inmates working in the prison kitchens). His seductive charm also seems miraculously sustained, and Johnson gravely reports how Savage makes a final conquest of his kindly gaoler, Mr Able Dagge. We may be sure that Mr Dagge also came to believe he was 'the son of the late Earl Rivers'.

In a surprising and effective move, Johnson for the first time uses long quotations from three of Savage's own letters to bring us most closely into his company. This is the section that Johnson re-wrote all night in January 1744 against his publisher's deadline, and shows how the prospect of immanent execution – as he later remarked in another context – wonderfully concentrates the writer's mind.

The first of these letters is to a Bristol friend, Saunders; the last evidently to his publisher, the faithful Edward Cave; the middle one is anonymous, 'to one of his friends in London'. In each we hear Savage's own voice, and experience his fantastic and violent shifts of mood – resignation, followed by fury, pride, bitterness, insouciance, despair, charm, enigmatic mystery. The changes are so volatile, so swift and so extreme, that one might almost think one was witnessing actual changes in Savage's personality – or identity. No doubt Johnson intended his readers to reflect on the psychological implications of that too.

It is possible that the confidential and touching middle letter, to the unnamed 'friend in London', was actually to Johnson himself. It has a stoic piety that Johnson would have admired. It also seems to make an unmistakable, rueful, smiling reference to their previous argument about the charms of rural life, and the amiable delusion of birds singing from every bramble.

Typically, Savage finds a delightful way of proving that young Johnson was wrong, and that he – Savage – was telling the truth all along. 'I thank the Almighty, I am now all collected in myself; and, though my person is in Confinement, my mind can expatiate on ample and useful subjects with all the freedom imaginable. I am now more conversant with the Nine than ever, and if, instead of a Newgate-bird, I am allowed to be a bird of the Muses, I assure you, Sir, I sing very freely in my Cage; sometimes, indeed, in the plaintive notes of the Nightingale; but at others in the cheerful strains of the Lark.' (p.95)

The end, when it comes, is swift but enigmatic. The dying Savage has one more secret to impart, but moving his hand 'in a melancholy manner', fails to tell it to his kindly gaoler – or to his attentive biographer. Johnson's elegant summary of Savage's extraordinary mixture of vices and virtues maintains its tender, ironic balance to the last. Although, not quite to the last. The final appeal is made directly to the reader's sympathy, to his heart, in what became Johnson's most celebrated biographical peroration. 'For his life, or for his writings, none who candidly consider his fortune, will think an apology either necessary or difficult ... Those are no proper judges of his conduct, who have slumbered away their time on the down of plenty; nor will any wise man presume to say, "Had I been in Savage's condition, I should have lived or written better than Savage."' (p.105)

There is in fact one more paragraph, which concludes with a more severe and conventional verdict, bringing the two words 'genius' and 'contemptible' into irreconcilable contact. But against this, Savage's friend and advocate later wrote dismissively in the margin of his own 1748 copy: 'Added'.

8

The biography was an immediate and dazzling success. It became the book of the season, the talk of the London coffee-houses, and the subject of ecstatic reviews. The monthly *Champion* was representative: 'This pamphlet is, without flattery to its [anonymous] author, as just and well written a piece of its kind I ever saw ... It is not only the story of Mr Savage, but innumerable incidents relating to other persons and other affairs, which renders this a very amusing and withal a very instructive and valuable performance ... The author's observations are short, significant and just...His reflections open to all the recesses of the human heart.' Johnson would particularly have liked that last phrase.

The reaction of the fashionable painter, Sir Joshua Reynolds, was typical of contemporary readers. He was delighted by the picturesque elements of Savage's story, and even more by Johnson's wonderfully shrewd comments and reflections. He did not question the historical truth of Savage's claims, but was simply gripped and mesmerized by its human drama. Reynolds told Boswell that 'upon his return from Italy he met with it in Devonshire, knowing nothing of its author, and began to read it while he was standing with his arm leaning against a chimney-piece. It seized his attention so strongly, that, not being able to lay down the book till he had finished it, when he attempted to move, he found his arm totally benumbed.'

Although anonymous, it would be true to say that the publication of the *Life of Richard Savage* in 1744 made Johnson's name, and determined him to continue as a professional author in London. He was 35, and from henceforth he began to sign his own books and poems. Within three years he was able to agree the contract for the *Dictionary*, with a substantial advance payment of £1,575 from a syndicate of London publishers, and take the famous house in Gough Square. A second edition of the *Life of Savage* was also published by Cave in 1748, and his greatest poem 'The Vanity of Human Wishes' followed in 1749. No doubt Savage would have been pleased by all this, and made one of his famous, hat-doffing bows to his young protegee.

Johnson's further reflections on Biography and Autobiography appear in three short essays, which are appended to this edition. In *Rambler* No. 60, 'On the Dignity and Usefulness of Biography' he made the first great modern defence of the form (1750). He argued both for its intimate nature, and its universal appeal, and enshrined these in some notable aphorisms. 'More knowledge may be gained of a man's real character, by a short conversation with one of his servants, than from a formal and studied narrative, begun with his pedigree, and ended with his funeral'. (p.114). He also raised the question of how far we can believe in autobiography; and suggested the particular value of literary biography, with its emphasis on inner imaginative drama. 'The gradations of a hero's life are from battle to battle; and an author's from book to book.' (p.126)

In after years Johnson often talked to Boswell about the nature and appeal of biography. In 1763, the year they met, he boasted that 'the biographical part of literature is what I love most.' Later in 1772, clearly thinking back to his time with Savage, he gave it as his opinion that 'nobody can write the life of a man, but those who have eat and drunk and lived in social intercourse with him.' But later still, in 1776, talking with Thomas Warton at Trinity College Cambridge, he added that even biography based on personal intimacy was 'rarely well executed ... Few people who have lived with a man know what to remark about him'. However, he never revived the question of the historical truth of Savage's claims in Boswell's hearing.

Yet, right or wrong, Johnson had done something normally associated with much later 20th century biography. He had made Savage's childhood and adolescence a determining factor in his adult struggles. Whether genuinely a rejected child, or a brilliant obsessive fraud, a tragic self-deluded impostor, Savage was defined by a 'lost' childhood identity. It would of course be anachronistic to talk of Freudian insights in an early 18th century text. But Johnson's treatment of Savage's obsession with his 'Cruel Mother' always repays further reading.

Beyond the historical controversy, it can be seen to yield remarkable psychological insights. Johnson noted, for example, that when the actress Anne Oldfield (with whom Savage may have had an affair) died in 1730, 'he endeavored to show his gratitude in the most decent manner, by wearing mourning as for a Mother.' (p.15). He also observed that throughout his adult life Savage should be 'considered as a child exposed to all the temptations of indigence'. (p.53). His final appeal is not for formal justice, but for the warmth of human understanding.

In a longer perspective, one can see that Johnson had championed English biography as a virtually new genre. He had saved it from the medieval tradition of solemnly extended hagiography, or the lifeless accumulations of 17th century biographical Dictionaries. He had shown that it was not 'compiled', but narrated, argued and brought dramatically alive. He had also raised it above those commercial compilations of scandalous anecdote, that were still so much in vogue, like Theophilus Cibber's *Lives of the Poets* (1753, 200 poets packed like sardines into 5 volumes).

He had separated it from gossip and cheap romance, and

redirected it towards 'the Lovers of Truth and Wit'. By introducing the subject's own writings – poetry, essays, letters – into the narrative, he had made it more scholarly and authentic. Nor was it any longer dependent on classical models and the lives of the great and eminent – as those by Plutarch, Tacitus, or Suetonius. Instead it had absorbed several popular and indigenous English forms – the Newgate confession, the sentimental ballad, the courtroom drama, even the Restoration comedy of manners.

Moreover English biography was no longer necessarily about fame and success. It could take obscure, failed and damaged lives, and make them intensely moving and revealing. Biography was an act of imaginative friendship, and depended on moral intelligence and human sympathy. Biography had become a new kind of narrative about the mysteries of the human heart.

Many years later Johnson is reported to have told Boswell, 'that he could write the Life of a Broomstick'.

Johnson made minor corrections to The Life of Richard Savage *in the second edition of 1748, and reduced the footnotes in the subsequent editions of 1775 and the definitive edition incorporated into* The Lives of the Eminent English Poets *of 1781. (See Select Chronology) The text used here is based on the 1781 edition, with some modernizing of capital letters and punctuation.*

SELECT CHRONOLOGY

1697/8 (16 January ?) Richard Savage born in Holborn, London
Brought up by a nurse as Richard Smith

1709 Samuel Johnson born in Lichfield, Staffordshire

1712 Death of the 4th Earl Rivers

1715 Richard Smith discovers 'convincing Original Letters' apparently proving his true birthright as Richard Savage

1716 Savage begins to haunt the street outside Lady Macclesfield's house

1718 Savage is befriended by Sir Richard Steele, and the Drury Lane actors Robert Wilks and Anne Oldfield.

1720 Savage receives a £50 pension from Ann Oldfield until her death

1723 Savage's play *Sir Thomas Overbury* fails at Drury Lane

1724 Aaron Hill begins campaign on behalf of Savage in the *Plain Dealer*, and publishes 'Lament'

1726 Savage publishes *Miscellaneous Poems*, with Preface violently attacking Lady Macclesfield

1727 (December) Trial of Savage, and conviction for murder
Publication of the anonymous pamphlet The *Life of Mr Richard Savage, Who was Convicted of Murder at the Old Bailey*

1728 Savage receives Royal Pardon
Savage publishes 'The Bastard' against Lady Macclesfield, which runs to five editions

Savage receives £200 pension from her nephew, Lord Tyrconnel

Savage's 'Golden' period begins

Johnson goes to Oxford University

1729   Savage publishes *The Wanderer*, dedicated to Lord Tyrconnel

1732   Savage appoints himself Volunteer Laureate to Queen Caroline, and receives £50 pension

1733   Savage begins publishing poetry in the *Gentleman's Magazine*

1735   Savage quarrels with Lord Tyrconnel, 'Right Honourable Brute and Booby' (Savage), and loses £200 pension

1736   Savage publishes *Of Public Spirit in Regard to Public Works*, dedicated to Frederick, Prince of Wales.

1737   (March) Johnson comes to London

Savage reprints 'The Bastard' in the *Gentleman's Magazine*

Savage meets Johnson at offices of *The Gentleman's Magazine*

(November) Death of Queen Caroline and loss of Savage's £50 pension

Savage reduced to penury

1738   Savage and Johnson begin to share night walks round London

(April) Johnson publishes Latin epigram in praise of Savage

(May) Johnson publishes poem *London*, partly based on Savage's experiences as 'Thales'

1739   Pope launches subscription scheme to support Savage in Wales with £50 pension

(July) Savage leaves for Bristol, parting from Johnson 'with Tears in his Eyes'.

1740   Savage in Wales

1743 (January) Savage arrested for debt in Bristol
      (1 August) Death of Richard Savage in Newgate Gaol,
      Bristol

1744 (February) Johnson publishes *An Account of the Life of
      Mr Richard Savage, Son of the Earl Rivers*

1748 Johnson publishes a second, corrected edition of the
      Life

1750 Johnson publishes 'On Biography' (*Rambler* No.60)

1753 Death of Lady Macclesfield (Mrs Ann Brett)

1759 Johnson publishes 'On Autobiography' (*Idler* No.84)

1760 Johnson publishes 'On Literary Biography' (*Idler*
      No.102)

1763 (May) Johnson meets James Boswell

1775 Publication of *The Works of Richard Savage Esq., with
      A Life by Samuel Johnson*, 2 vols.

1781 *Life of Mr Richard Savage* incorporated into *The Lives
      of the Most Eminent English Poets*

1784 Death of Samuel Johnson

1791 Boswell publishes *The Life of Samuel Johnson LL.D.*

AN ACCOUNT OF
THE LIFE OF
MR. RICHARD SAVAGE,
SON OF THE
EARL RIVERS

It has been observed in all ages that the advantages of nature or of fortune have contributed very little to the promotion of happiness; and that those whom the splendour of their rank, or the extent of their capacity have placed upon the summits of human life, have not often given any just occasion to envy, in those who look up to them from a lower station: whether it be that apparent superiority incites great designs, and great designs are naturally liable to fatal miscarriages; or, that the general lot of mankind is misery, and the misfortunes of those whose eminence drew upon them an universal attention, have been more carefully recorded, because they were more generally observed, and have in reality been only more conspicuous than those of others, not more frequent or more severe.

That affluence and power, advantages extrinsick and adventitious, and therefore easily separable from those by whom they are possessed, should very often flatter the mind with expectations of felicity which they cannot give, raises no astonishment; but it seems rational to hope, that intellectual greatness should produce better effects; that minds qualified for great attainments should first endeavour their own benefit; and that they, who are most able to teach others the way to happiness, should with most certainty follow it themselves.

But this expectation, however plausible, has been very frequently disappointed. The heroes of literary as well as civil history, have been very often no less remarkable for what they have suffered, than for what they have achieved; and volumes have been written only to enumerate the miseries of the learned, and relate their unhappy lives and untimely deaths.

To these mournful narratives, I am about to add the life of Richard Savage, a man whose writings entitle him to an eminent rank in the classes of learning, and whose misfortunes claim a degree of compassion, not always due to the unhappy, as they were often the consequences of the crimes of others, rather than his own.

In the year 1697, Anne, countess of Macclesfield, having lived for some time upon very uneasy terms with her husband, thought a publick confession of adultery the most obvious and expeditious method of obtaining her liberty; and therefore declared that the child, with which she was then great, was begotten by the Earl Rivers. This, as may be imagined, made her husband no less desirous of a separation than herself, and he prosecuted his design in the most effectual manner; for he applied not to the ecclesiastical courts for a divorce, but to the Parliament for an act, by which his marriage might be dissolved, the nuptial contract totally annulled, and the children of his wife illegitimated. This act, after the usual deliberation, he obtained, though without the approbation of some, who considered marriage as an affair only cognizable by ecclesiastical judges; and on March 3rd was separated from his wife, whose fortune, which was very great, was repaid her, and who having as well as her husband the liberty of making another choice was in a short time married to colonel Brett.

While the Earl of Macclesfield was prosecuting this affair his wife was on the 10th of January 1697–8 delivered of a son; and the Earl Rivers, by appearing to consider him as his own, left none any reason to doubt of the sincerity of her declaration; for he was his godfather and gave him his own name which was, by his direction, inserted in the register of St Andrew's parish in Holborn but, unfortunately, left him to the care of his mother, whom, as she was now set free from her husband, he probably imagined likely to treat with great tenderness the child that had contributed to so pleasing an event. It is not indeed easy to discover what motives could be found to overbalance that natural affection of a parent, or what interest could be promoted by neglect or cruelty. The dread of shame or of poverty, by which some wretches have been incited to abandon or to murder their children, cannot be supposed to have affected a woman who had proclaimed her crimes and solicited reproach, and on whom the clemency of the legislature had undeservedly bestowed a fortune, which would have been very little diminished by the expenses which the care of her child could have brought upon her. It was therefore not likely that she would be wicked without temptation; that she would look upon her son, from his birth, with a kind of resentment and abhorrence; and, instead of supporting, assisting, and defending him, delight to see him struggling with misery, or that she would take every opportunity of aggravating his misfortunes, and obstructing his resources, and, with an implacable and restless cruelty, continue her persecution from the first hour of his life to the last.

But, whatever were her motives, no sooner was her son born, than she discovered a resolution of disowning him; and in a very short time removed him from her sight, by committing him to the care of a poor woman, whom she directed to educate him as her own, and enjoined never to inform him of his true parents.

Such was the beginning of the life of Richard Savage. Born with a legal claim to honour and to affluence, he was, in two months, illegitimated by the Parliament, and disowned by his mother, doomed to poverty and obscurity, and launched upon the ocean of life, only that he might be swallowed by its quicksands, or dashed upon its rocks.

His mother could not indeed infect others with the same cruelty. As it was impossible to avoid the inquiries which the curiosity or tenderness of her relations made after her child, she was obliged to give some account of the measures she had taken; and her mother, the Lady Mason, whether in approbation of her design, or to prevent more criminal contrivances, engaged to transact with the nurse, to pay her for her care, and to superintend the education of the child.

In this charitable office she was assisted by his godmother, Mrs Lloyd, who, while she lived, always looked upon him with that tenderness which the barbarity of his mother made peculiarly necessary; but her death, which happened in his tenth year, was another of the misfortunes of his childhood; for though she kindly endeavoured to alleviate his loss by a legacy of three hundred pounds, yet, as he had none to prosecute his claim, to shelter him from oppression or call in law to the assistance of justice, her will was eluded by the executors and no part of the money was ever paid.

He was, however, not yet wholly abandoned. The Lady Mason still continued her care, and directed him to be placed at a small grammar-school near St Alban's, where he was called by the name of his nurse, without the least intimation that he had a claim to any other.

Here he was initiated in literature, and passed through several of the classes, with what rapidity or with what applause cannot now be known. As he always spoke with respect of his master, it is probable that the mean rank, in which he then appeared, did not hinder his genius from being distinguished, or his industry from being rewarded; and if in so low a state he obtained distinction and rewards, it is not likely they were gained but by genius and industry.

It is very reasonable to conjecture that his application was equal to his abilities because his improvement was more than proportioned to the opportunities which he enjoyed; nor can it be doubted that if his earliest productions had been preserved, like those of happier students, we might in some have found vigorous sallies of that sprightly humour which distinguishes the *Author to be Let*, and in others strong touches of that ardent imagination which painted the solemn scenes of the *Wanderer*.

While he was thus cultivating his genius his father, the Earl Rivers, was seized with a distemper which, in a short time, put an end to his life. He had frequently inquired after his son, and had always been amused with fallacious and evasive answers; but, being now, in his own opinion, on his deathbed he thought it his duty to provide for him among his other natural children, and therefore demanded a positive account of him with an importunity not to be diverted or denied. His mother, who could no longer refuse an answer determined at least to give such as should cut him off for ever from that happiness which competence affords and therefore declared that he was dead; which is perhaps the first instance of a lie invented by a mother to deprive her son of a provision which was designed him by another, and which she could not expect herself, though he should lose it.

This was therefore an act of wickedness which could not be defeated because it could not be suspected; the earl did not imagine there could exist in a human form a mother that would ruin her son without enriching herself, and therefore bestowed upon some other person six thousand pounds, which he had in his will bequeathed to Savage.

The same cruelty which incited his mother to intercept this provision which had been intended him prompted her, in a short time, to another project, a project worthy of such a disposition. She endeavoured to rid herself from the danger of being at any time made known to him by sending him secretly to the American plantations.

By whose kindness this scheme was counteracted, or by what interposition she was induced to lay aside her design, I know not; it is not improbable that the Lady Mason might persuade or compel her to desist, or perhaps she could not easily find accomplices wicked enough to concur in so cruel an action; for it may be conceived that those who had, by a long gradation of guilt, hardened their hearts against the sense of common wickedness, would yet be shocked at the design of a mother to expose her son to slavery and want, to expose him without interest, and without provocation; and Savage might, on this occasion, find protectors and advocates among those who had long traded in crimes, and whom compassion had never touched before.

Being hindered, by whatever means, from banishing him into another country, she formed soon after a scheme for burying him in poverty and obscurity in his own; and, that his station of life, if not the place of his residence, might keep him for ever at a distance from her, she ordered him to be placed with a shoemaker in Holborn that, after the usual time of trial, he might become his apprentice.

It is generally reported, that this project was for some time successful, and that Savage was employed at the awl longer than he was willing to confess; nor was it perhaps any great advantage to him that an unexpected discovery determined him to quit his occupation.

About this time his nurse, who had always treated him as her own son, died; and it was natural for him to take care of those effects which by her death were, as he imagined, become his own: he therefore went to her house, opened her boxes, and examined her papers, among which he found some letters written to her by the Lady Mason, which informed him of his birth, and the reasons for which it was concealed.

He was no longer satisfied with the employment which had been allotted him, but thought he had a right to share the affluence of his mother; and therefore without scruple applied to her as her son, and made use of every art to awaken her tenderness and attract her regard. But neither his letters, nor the interposition of those friends which his merit or his distress procured him, made any impression upon her mind. She still resolved to neglect, though she could no longer disown him.

It was to no purpose that he frequently solicited her to admit him to see her: she avoided him with the most vigilant precaution, and ordered him to be excluded from her house, by whomsoever he might be introduced, and what reason soever he might give for entering it.

Savage was at the same time so touched with the discovery of his real mother that it was his frequent practice to walk in the dark evenings for several hours before her door, in hopes of seeing her as she might come by accident to the window, or cross her apartment with a candle in her hand.

But all his assiduity and tenderness were without effect, for he could neither soften her heart nor open her hand, and was reduced to the utmost miseries of want, while he was endeavouring to awaken the affection of a mother. He was therefore obliged to seek some other means of support; and, having no profession, became by necessity an author.

At this time the attention of the literary world was engrossed by the Bangorian controversy, which filled the press with pamphlets, and the coffee-houses with disputants. Of this subject, as most popular, he made choice for his first attempt and, without any other knowledge of the question than he had casually collected from conversation, published a poem against the bishop.

What was the success or merit of this performance I know not; it was probably lost among the innumerable pamphlets to which that dispute gave occasion. Mr Savage was himself in a little time ashamed of it, and endeavoured to suppress it, by destroying all the copies that he could collect.

He then attempted a more gainful kind of writing and, in his eighteenth year, offered to the stage a comedy borrowed from a Spanish plot, which was refused by the players, and was therefore given by him to Mr Bullock, who, having more interest, made some slight alterations, and brought it upon the stage, under the title of *Woman's a Riddle*, but allowed the unhappy author no part of the profit.

Not discouraged however at his repulse, he wrote, two years afterwards, *Love in a Veil*, another comedy, borrowed likewise from the Spanish, but with little better success than before; for, though it was received and acted, yet it appeared so late in the year that the author obtained no other advantage from it than the acquaintance of Sir Richard Steele, and Mr Wilks, by whom he was pitied, caressed, and relieved.

Sir Richard Steele, having declared in his favour with all the ardour of benevolence which constituted his character, promoted his interest with the utmost zeal, related his misfortunes, applauded his merit, took all the opportunities of recommending him, and asserted that 'the inhumanity of his mother had given him a right to find every good man his father.'

Nor was Mr Savage admitted to his acquaintance only, but to his confidence, of which he sometimes related an instance too extraordinary to be omitted, as it affords a very just idea of his patron's character.

He was once desired by Sir Richard, with an air of the utmost importance, to come very early to his house the next morning. Mr Savage came as he had promised, found the chariot at the door, and Sir Richard waiting for him and ready to go out. What was intended, and whither they were to go, Savage could not conjecture, and was not willing to inquire; but immediately seated himself with Sir Richard. The coachman was ordered to drive, and they hurried, with the utmost expedition, to Hyde-Park corner, where they stopped at a petty tavern and retired to a private room. Sir Richard then informed him, that he intended to publish a pamphlet and that he had desired him to come thither that he might write for him. They soon sat down to the work. Sir Richard dictated, and Savage wrote, till the dinner that had been ordered was put upon the table. Savage was surprised at the meanness of the entertainment, and, after some hesitation, ventured to ask for wine, which Sir Richard, not without reluctance, ordered to be brought. They then finished their dinner, and proceeded in their pamphlet, which they concluded in the afternoon.

Mr Savage then imagined his task over, and expected that Sir Richard would call for the reckoning, and return home; but his expectations deceived him, for Sir Richard told him that he was without money, and that the pamphlet must be sold, before the dinner could be paid for; and Savage was therefore obliged to go and offer their new production to sale for two guineas, which with some difficulty he obtained. Sir Richard then returned home, having retired that day only to avoid his creditors, and composed the pamphlet only to discharge his reckoning.

Mr Savage related another fact equally uncommon, which, though it has no relation to his life, ought to be preserved. Sir Richard Steele having one day invited to his house a great number of persons of the first quality, they were surprised at the number of liveries which surrounded the table; and after dinner, when wine and mirth had set them free from the observation of rigid ceremony, one of them inquired of Sir Richard, how such an expensive train of domesticks could be consistent with his fortune. Sir Richard very frankly confessed that they were fellows of whom he would very willingly be rid: and being then asked why he did not discharge them, declared that they were bailiffs, who had introduced themselves with an execution, and whom, since he could not send them away, he had thought it convenient to embellish with liveries that they might do him credit while they staid.

His friends were diverted with the expedient, and, by paying the debt, discharged their attendance, having obliged Sir Richard to promise that they should never again find him graced with a retinue of the same kind.

Under such a tutor Mr Savage was not likely to learn prudence or frugality; and perhaps many of the misfortunes which the want of those virtues brought upon him in the following parts of his life, might be justly imputed to so unimproving an example.

Nor did the kindness of Sir Richard end in common favours. He proposed to have established him in some settled scheme of life, and to have contracted a kind of alliance with him by marrying him to a natural daughter, on whom he intended to bestow a thousand pounds. But, though he was always lavish of future bounties, he conducted his affairs in such a manner that he was very seldom able to keep his promises, or execute his own intentions; and, as he was never able to raise the sum which he had offered, the marriage was delayed. In the mean time he was officiously informed that Mr Savage had ridiculed him; by which he was so much exasperated that he withdrew the allowance which he had paid him, and never afterwards admitted him to his house.

It is not indeed unlikely that Savage might, by his imprudence, expose himself to the malice of a talebearer; for his patron had many follies, which, as his discernment easily discovered, his imagination might sometimes incite him to mention too ludicrously. A little knowledge of the world is sufficient to discover that such weakness is very common, and that there are few who do not sometimes, in the wantonness of thoughtless mirth, or the heat of transient resentment, speak of their friends and benefactors with levity and contempt, though, in their cooler moments, they want neither sense of their kindness, nor reverence for their virtue: the fault therefore of Mr Savage was rather negligence than ingratitude. But Sir Richard must, likewise, be acquitted of severity, for who is there that can patiently bear contempt from one whom he has relieved and supported, whose establishment he has laboured, and whose interest he has promoted?

He was now again abandoned to fortune, without any other friend than Mr Wilks; a man who, whatever were his abilities or skill as an actor, deserves at least to be remembered for his virtues, which are not often to be found in the world, and perhaps less often in his profession than in others. To be humane, generous, and candid, is a very high degree of merit in any case; but those qualities deserve still greater praise when they are found in that condition which makes almost every other man, for whatever reason, contemptuous, insolent, petulant, selfish, and brutal.

As Mr Wilks was one of those to whom calamity seldom complained without relief, he naturally took an unfortunate wit into his protection, and not only assisted him in any casual distresses, but continued an equal and steady kindness to the time of his death.

By his interposition Mr Savage once obtained from his mother fifty pounds, and a promise of one hundred and fifty more; but it was the fate of this unhappy man that few promises of any advantage to him were performed. His mother was infected, among others, with the general madness of the South-sea traffick; and, having been disappointed in her expectations, refused to pay what perhaps nothing but the prospect of sudden affluence prompted her to promise.

Being thus obliged to depend upon the friendship of Mr Wilks he was, consequently, an assiduous frequenter of the theatres; and, in a short time, the amusements of the stage took such possession of his mind, that he never was absent from a play in several years.

This constant attendance naturally procured him the acquaintance of the players; and, among others, of Mrs Oldfield, who was so much pleased with his conversation, and touched with his misfortunes, that she allowed him a settled pension of fifty pounds a year, which was during her life regularly paid.

That this act of generosity may receive its due praise, and that the good actions of Mrs Oldfield may not be sullied by her general character, it is proper to mention what Mr Savage often declared, in the strongest terms, that he never saw her alone, or in any other place than behind the scenes.

At her death he endeavoured to show his gratitude in the most decent manner, by wearing mourning, as for a mother; but did not celebrate her in elegies, because he knew that too great profusion of praise would only have revived those faults which his natural equity did not allow him to think less, because they were committed by one who favoured him; but of which, though his virtue would not endeavour to palliate them, his gratitude would not suffer him to prolong the memory, or diffuse the censure.

In his *Wanderer*, he has indeed taken an opportunity of mentioning her; but celebrates her not for her virtue, but her beauty, an excellence which none ever denied her: this is the only encomium with which he has rewarded her liberality; and perhaps he has, even in this, been too lavish of his praise. He seems to have thought, that never to mention his benefactress would have an appearance of ingratitude, though to have dedicated any particular performance to her memory would have only betrayed an officious partiality, that, without exalting her character, would have depressed his own.

He had sometimes, by the kindness of Mr Wilks, the advantage of a benefit, on which occasions he often received uncommon marks of regard and compassion; and was once told, by the Duke of Dorset, that it was just to consider him as an injured nobleman; and that, in his opinion, the nobility ought to think themselves obliged, without solicitation, to take every opportunity of supporting him by their countenance and patronage. But he had generally the mortification to hear that the whole interest of his mother was employed to frustrate his applications, and that she never left any expedient untried, by which he might be cut off from the possibility of supporting life. The same disposition she endeavoured to diffuse among all those over whom nature or fortune gave her any influence; and indeed succeeded too well in her design; but could not always propagate her effrontery with her cruelty; for some of those, whom she incited against him, were ashamed of their own conduct, and boasted of that relief which they never gave him.

In this censure I do not indiscriminately involve all his relations; for he has mentioned, with gratitude, the humanity of one lady, whose name I am now unable to recollect, and to whom therefore I cannot pay the praises which she deserves, for having acted well in opposition to influence, precept, and example.

The punishment which our laws inflict upon those parents who murder their infants is well known; nor has its justice ever been contested; but, if they deserve death who destroy a child in its birth, what pains can be severe enough for her who forbears to destroy him, only to inflict sharper miseries upon him; who prolongs his life, only to make him miserable; and who exposes him, without care and without pity, to the malice of oppression, the caprices of chance, and the temptations of poverty; who rejoices to see him overwhelmed with calamities; and, when his own industry, or the charity of others, has enabled him to rise, for a short time, above his miseries, plunges him again into his former distress?

The kindness of his friends not affording him any constant supply, and the prospect of improving his fortune by enlarging his acquaintance necessarily leading him to places of expense, he found it necessary to endeavour, once more, at dramatick poetry, for which he was now better qualified, by a more exten-

sive knowledge and longer observation. But having been unsuccessful in comedy, though rather for want of opportunities than
genius, he resolved now to try whether he should not be more
fortunate in exhibiting a tragedy.

The story which he chose for the subject was that of Sir
Thomas Overbury, a story well adapted to the stage, though
perhaps not far enough removed from the present age to admit
properly the fictions necessary to complete the plan; for the
mind, which naturally loves truth, is always most offended with
the violation of those truths of which we are most certain; and
we of course conceive those facts most certain which approach
nearest to our own time.

Out of this story he formed a tragedy, which, if the circumstances in which he wrote it be considered, will afford at once
an uncommon proof of strength of genius, and evenness of mind,
of a serenity not to be ruffled, and an imagination not to be
suppressed.

During a considerable part of the time in which he was
employed upon this performance, he was without lodging, and
often without meat; nor had he any other conveniencies for
study than the fields or the streets allowed him: there he used
to walk and form his speeches, and afterwards step into a shop,
beg for a few moments the use of the pen and ink, and write
down what he had composed upon paper which he had picked
up by accident.

If the performance of a writer thus distressed is not perfect,
its faults ought surely to be imputed to a cause very different
from want of genius, and must rather excite pity than provoke
censure.

But when, under these discouragements, the tragedy was
finished there yet remained the labour of introducing it on the

stage; an undertaking, which, to an ingenuous mind, was, in a very high degree, vexatious and disgusting; for, having little interest or reputation, he was obliged to submit himself wholly to the players, and admit, with whatever reluctance, the emendations of Mr Cibber, which he always considered as the disgrace of his performance.

He had indeed in Mr Hill another critick of a very different class, from whose friendship he received great assistance on many occasions, and whom he never mentioned but with the utmost tenderness and regard. He had been for some time distinguished by him with very particular kindness, and on this occasion it was natural to apply to him, as an author of an established character. He therefore sent this tragedy to him, with a short copy of verses, in which he desired his correction. Mr Hill, whose humanity and politeness are generally known, readily complied with his request; but, as he is remarkable for singularity of sentiment, and bold experiments in language, Mr Savage did not think his play much improved by his innovation, and had, even at that time, the courage to reject several passages which he could not approve; and, what is still more laudable, Mr Hill had the generosity not to resent the neglect of his alterations, but wrote the prologue and epilogue, in which he touches on the circumstances of the author with great tenderness.

After all these obstructions and compliances, he was only able to bring his play upon the stage in the summer, when the chief actors had retired, and the rest were in possession of the house for their own advantage. Among these, Mr Savage was admitted to play the part of Sir Thomas Overbury, by which he gained no great reputation, the theatre being a province for which nature seemed not to have designed him; for neither his voice, look, nor gesture, were such as were expected on the stage; and he was so much ashamed of having been reduced to appear as a player, that he always blotted out his name from the list, when a copy of his tragedy was to be shown to his friends.

In the publication of his performance he was more successful, for the rays of genius that glimmered in it, that glimmered through all the mists which poverty and Cibber had been able to spread over it, procured him the notice and esteem of many persons eminent for their rank, their virtue, and their wit.

Of this play, acted, printed, and dedicated, the accumulated profits arose to a hundred pounds, which he thought at that time a very large sum, having been never master of so much before.

In the dedication, for which he received ten guineas, there is nothing remarkable. The preface contains a very liberal encomium on the blooming excellencies of Mr Theophilus Cibber, which Mr Savage could not in the latter part of his life see his friends about to read without snatching the play out of their hands. The generosity of Mr Hill did not end on this occasion; for afterwards, when Mr Savage's necessities returned, he encouraged a subscription to a *Miscellany of Poems* in a very extraordinary manner, by publishing his story in the *Plain Dealer*, with some affecting lines, which he asserts to have been written by Mr Savage upon the treatment received by him from his mother, but of which he was himself the author, as Mr Savage afterwards declared. These lines, and the paper in which they were inserted, had a very powerful effect upon all but his mother, whom, by making her cruelty more publick, they only hardened in her aversion.

Mr Hill not only promoted the subscription to the *Miscellany*, but furnished likewise the greatest part of the poems of which it is composed, and particularly the 'Happy Man', which he published as a specimen.

The subscriptions of those whom these papers should influence to patronise merit in distress, without any other solicitation, were directed to be left at Button's coffee-house; and Mr Savage going thither a few days afterwards, without expectation of any effect from his proposal, found to his surprise seventy guineas, which had been sent him in consequence of the compassion excited by Mr Hill's pathetick representation.

To this *Miscellany* he wrote a preface, in which he gives an account of his mother's cruelty in a very uncommon strain of humour, and with a gaiety of imagination, which the success of his subscription probably produced.

The dedication is addressed to the Lady Mary Wortley Montague, whom he flatters without reserve, and, to confess the truth, with very little art. The same observation may be extended to all his dedications: his compliments are constrained and violent, heaped together without the grace of order, or the decency of introduction: he seems to have written his panegyricks for the perusal only of his patrons, and to have imagined that he had no other task than to pamper them with praises, however gross, and that flattery would make its way to the heart, without the assistance of elegance or invention.

Soon afterwards the death of the king furnished a general subject for a poetical contest, in which Mr Savage engaged, and is allowed to have carried the prize of honour from his competitors: but I know not whether he gained by his performance any other advantage than the increase of his reputation; though it must certainly have been with further views that he prevailed upon himself to attempt a species of writing, of which all the topicks had been long before exhausted, and which was made at once difficult by the multitudes that had failed in it, and those that had succeeded.

He was now advancing in reputation, and though frequently involved in very distressful perplexities, appeared however to be gaining upon mankind, when both his fame and his life were endangered by an event, of which it is not yet determined, whether it ought to be mentioned as a crime or a calamity.

On the 20th of November 1727 Mr Savage came from Richmond, where he then lodged, that he might pursue his studies with less interruption, with an intent to discharge another lodging which he had in Westminster; and accidentally meeting two gentlemen, his acquaintances, whose names were Merchant and Gregory, he went in with them to a neighbouring coffee-house, and sat drinking till it was late, it being in no time of Mr Savage's life any part of his character to be the first of the company that desired to separate. He would willingly have gone to bed in the same house; but there was not room for the whole company, and therefore they agreed to ramble about the streets, and divert themselves with such amusements as should offer themselves till morning.

In this walk they happened unluckily to discover a light in Robinson's coffee-house, near Charing-Cross, and therefore went in. Merchant, with some rudeness, demanded a room, and was told that there was a good fire in the next parlour, which the company were about to leave, being then paying their reckoning. Merchant, not satisfied with this answer, rushed into the room, and was followed by his companions. He then petulantly placed himself between the company and the fire, and soon after kicked down the table. This produced a quarrel, swords were drawn on both sides, and one Mr James Sinclair was killed. Savage, having likewise wounded a maid that held him, forced his way with Merchant out of the house; but being intimidated and confused, without resolution either to fly or stay, they were taken in a back court by one of the company, and some soldiers, whom he had called to his assistance.

Being secured and guarded that night, they were in the morning carried before three justices, who committed them to the Gate-house, from whence, upon the death of Mr Sinclair, which happened the same day, they were removed in the night to Newgate, where they were however treated with some distinction, exempted from the ignominy of chains, and confined, not among the common criminals, but in the press-yard.

When the day of trial came, the court was crowded in a very unusual manner; and the publick appeared to interest itself, as in a cause of general concern. The witnesses against Mr Savage and his friends were the woman who kept the house, which was a house of ill fame, and her maid, the men who were in the room with Mr Sinclair, and a woman of the town, who had been drinking with them, and with whom one of them had been seen in bed. They swore in general that Merchant gave the provocation, which Savage and Gregory drew their swords to justify; that Savage drew first, and that he stabbed Sinclair when he was not in a posture of defence, or while Gregory commanded his sword; that after he had given the thrust he turned pale, and would have retired, but that the maid clung round him, and one of the company endeavoured to detain him, from whom he broke, by cutting the maid on the head, but was afterwards taken in a court.

There was some difference in their depositions; one did not see Savage give the wound, another saw it given when Sinclair held his point towards the ground; and the woman of the town asserted that she did not see Sinclair's sword at all: this difference however was very far from amounting to inconsistency; but it was sufficient to show that the hurry of the dispute was such that it was not easy to discover the truth with relation to particular circumstances, and that therefore some deductions were to be made from the credibility of the testimonies.

Sinclair had declared several times before his death that he received his wound from Savage; nor did Savage at his trial deny the fact, but endeavoured partly to extenuate it by urging the suddenness of the whole action, and the impossibility of any ill design, or premeditated malice; and partly to justify it by the necessity of self-defence, and the hazard of his own life, if he had lost that opportunity of giving the thrust: he observed, that neither reason nor law obliged a man to wait for the blow which was threatened, and which, if he should suffer it, he might never be able to return; that it was always allowable to prevent an assault, and to preserve life by taking away that of the adversary by whom it was endangered.

With regard to the violence with which he endeavoured to escape, he declared, that it was not his design to fly from justice, or decline a trial, but to avoid the expenses and severities of a prison; and that he intended to have appeared at the bar without compulsion.

This defence, which took up more than an hour, was heard by the multitude that thronged the court with the most attentive and respectful silence; those who thought he ought not to be acquitted owned that applause could not be refused him; and those who before pitied his misfortunes now reverenced his abilities.

The witnesses which appeared against him were proved to be persons of characters which did not entitle them to much credit; a common strumpet, a woman by whom strumpets were entertained, and a man by whom they were supported: and the character of Savage was, by several persons of distinction, asserted to be that of a modest inoffensive man, not inclined to broils or to insolence, and who had, to that time, been only known for his misfortunes and his wit.

Had his audience been his judges, he had undoubtedly been acquitted; but Mr Page, who was then upon the bench, treated him with his usual insolence and severity, and when he had summed up the evidence, endeavoured to exasperate the jury, as Mr Savage used to relate it, with this eloquent harangue:

'Gentlemen of the jury, you are to consider that Mr Savage is a very great man, a much greater man than you or I, gentlemen of the jury; that he wears very fine clothes, much finer clothes than you or I, gentlemen of the jury; that he has abundance of money in his pocket, much more money than you or I, gentlemen of the jury; but, gentlemen of the jury, is it not a very hard case, gentlemen of the jury, that Mr Savage should therefore kill you or me, gentlemen of the jury?'

Mr Savage, hearing his defence thus misrepresented, and the men who were to decide his fate incited against him by invidious comparisons, resolutely asserted, that his cause was not candidly explained, and began to recapitulate what he had before said with regard to his condition, and the necessity of endeavouring to escape the expenses of imprisonment; but the judge having ordered him to be silent, and repeated his orders without effect, commanded that he should be taken from the bar by force.

The jury then heard the opinion of the judge, that good characters were of no weight against positive evidence, though they might turn the scale where it was doubtful; and that though, when two men attack each other, the death of either is only manslaughter; but where one is the aggressor, as in the case before them, and, in pursuance of his first attack, kills the other, the law supposes the action, however sudden, to be malicious.

They then deliberated upon their verdict, and determined that Mr Savage and Mr Gregory were guilty of murder; and Mr Merchant, who had no sword, only of manslaughter.

Thus ended this memorable trial, which lasted eight hours. Mr Savage and Mr Gregory were conducted back to prison, where they were more closely confined, and loaded with irons of fifty pounds' weight: four days afterwards they were sent back to the court to receive sentence; on which occasion Mr Savage made, as far as it could be retained in memory, the following speech:

'It is now, my lord, too late to offer any thing by way of defence or vindication; nor can we expect from your lordships, in this court, but the sentence which the law requires you, as judges, to pronounce against men of our calamitous condition. But we are also persuaded, that as mere men, and out of this seat of rigorous justice, you are susceptive of the tender passions, and too humane not to commiserate the unhappy situation of those, whom the law sometimes perhaps – exacts – from you to pronounce upon. No doubt, you distinguish between offences which arise out of premeditation, and a disposition habituated to vice or immorality, and transgressions, which are the unhappy and unforeseen effects of casual absence of reason, and sudden impulse of passion; we therefore hope you will contribute all you can to an extension of that mercy, which the gentlemen of the jury have been pleased to show Mr Merchant, who (allowing facts as sworn against us by the evidence) has led us into this our calamity. I hope this will not be construed as if we meant to reflect upon that gentleman, or remove any thing from us upon him, or that we repine the more at our fate, because he has no participation of it: no, my lord; for my part, I declare nothing could more soften my grief, than to be without any companion in so great a misfortune.'

Mr Savage had now no hopes of life, but from the mercy of the crown, which was very earnestly solicited by his friends, and which, with whatever difficulty the story may obtain belief, was obstructed only by his mother.

To prejudice the Queen against him, she made use of an incident, which was omitted in the order of time, that it might be mentioned together with the purpose which it was made to serve. Mr Savage, when he had discovered his birth, had an incessant desire to speak to his mother, who always avoided him in publick, and refused him admission into her house. One evening walking, as it was his custom, in the street that she inhabited, he saw the door of her house by accident open; he entered it and, finding no person in the passage to hinder him, went up stairs to salute her. She discovered him before he could enter her chamber, alarmed the family with the most distressful outcries and, when she had by her screams gathered them about her, ordered them to drive out of the house that villain, who had forced himself in upon her and endeavoured to murder her. Savage, who had attempted, with the most submissive tenderness, to soften her rage, hearing her utter so detestable an accusation, thought it prudent to retire; and I believe never attempted afterwards to speak to her.

But, shocked as he was with her falsehood and her cruelty, he imagined that she intended no other use of her lie, than to set herself free from his embraces and solicitations, and was very far from suspecting that she would treasure it in her memory as an instrument of future wickedness, or that she would endeavour for this fictitious assault to deprive him of his life.

But when the Queen was solicited for his pardon, and informed of the severe treatment which he had suffered from his judge, she answered that, however unjustifiable might be the manner of his trial, or whatever extenuation the action for which he was condemned might admit, she could not think that man a proper object of the king's mercy, who had been capable of entering his mother's house in the night with an intent to murder her.

By whom this atrocious calumny had been transmitted to the queen; whether she that invented had the front to relate it; whether she found any one weak enough to credit it, or corrupt enough to concur with her in her hateful design, I know not; but methods had been taken to persuade the queen so strongly of the truth of it that she for a long time refused to hear any of those who petitioned for his life.

Thus had Savage perished by the evidence of a bawd, a strumpet, and his mother, had not justice and compassion procured him an advocate of rank too great to be rejected unheard, and of virtue too eminent to be heard without being believed. His merit and his calamities happened to reach the ear of the Countess of Hertford, who engaged in his support with all the tenderness that is excited by pity, and all the zeal which is kindled by generosity; and, demanding an audience of the queen, laid before her the whole series of his mother's cruelty, exposed the improbability of an accusation by which he was charged with an intent to commit a murder that could produce no advantage, and soon convinced her how little his former conduct could deserve to be mentioned as a reason for extraordinary severity.

The interposition of this lady was so successful that he was soon after admitted to bail, and, on the 9th of March, 1728, pleaded the king's pardon.

It is natural to inquire upon what motives his mother could prosecute him in a manner so outrageous and implacable; for what reason she could employ all the arts of malice and all the snares of calumny to take away the life of her own son, of a son who never injured her, who was never supported by her expense, nor obstructed any prospect of pleasure or advantage: why she should endeavour to destroy him by a lie – a lie which could not gain credit, but must vanish of itself at the first moment of examination, and of which only this can be said to make it probable, that it may be observed from her conduct that the most execrable crimes are sometimes committed without apparent temptation.

This mother is still alive, and may, perhaps, even yet, though her malice was so often defeated, enjoy the pleasure of reflecting, that the life, which she often endeavoured to destroy, was, at least, shortened by her maternal offices; that, though she could not transport her son to the plantations, bury him in the shop of a mechanick, or hasten the hand of the publick executioner, she has yet had the satisfaction of imbittering all his hours, and forcing him into exigencies that hurried on his death.

It is by no means necessary to aggravate the enormity of this woman's conduct, by placing it in opposition to that of the countess of Hertford; no one can fail to observe how much more amiable it is to relieve, than to oppress, and to rescue innocence from destruction, than to destroy without an injury.

Mr Savage, during his imprisonment, his trial, and the time in which he lay under sentence of death, behaved with great firmness and equality of mind, and confirmed by his fortitude the esteem of those who before admired him for his abilities. The peculiar circumstances of his life were made more generally known by a short account, which was then published, and of which several thousands were, in a few weeks, dispersed over the nation; and the compassion of mankind operated so powerfully in his favour, that he was enabled, by frequent presents, not only to support himself, but to assist Mr Gregory in prison;

and, when he was pardoned and released, he found the number of his friends not lessened.

The nature of the act for which he had been tried was in itself doubtful; of the evidences which appeared against him, the character of the man was not unexceptionable, that of the woman notoriously infamous; she, whose testimony chiefly influenced the jury to condemn him, afterwards retracted her assertions. He always himself denied that he was drunk, as had been generally reported. Mr Gregory, who is now, 1744, Collector of Antigua, is said to declare him far less criminal than he was imagined, even by some who favoured him; and Page himself afterwards confessed, that he had treated him with uncommon rigour. When all these particulars are rated together, perhaps the memory of Savage may not be much sullied by his trial.

Some time after he had obtained his liberty, he met in the street the woman that had sworn with so much malignity against him. She informed him that she was in distress and, with a degree of confidence not easily attainable, desired him to relieve her. He, instead of insulting her misery, and taking pleasure in the calamities of one who had brought his life into danger, reproved her gently for her perjury; and changing the only guinea that he had, divided it equally between her and himself.

This is an action which, in some ages, would have made a saint, and perhaps in others a hero, and which, without any hyperbolical encomiums, must be allowed to be an instance of uncommon generosity, an act of complicated virtue; by which he at once relieved the poor, corrected the vicious, and forgave an enemy; by which he at once remitted the strongest provocations, and exercised the most ardent charity.

Compassion was, indeed, the distinguishing quality of Savage; he never appeared inclined to take advantage of weakness, to attack the defenceless, or to press upon the falling: whoever was distressed, was certain at least of his good wishes; and when he could give no assistance to extricate them from misfortunes, he endeavoured to sooth them by sympathy and tenderness.

But when his heart was not softened by the sight of misery, he was sometimes obstinate in his resentment, and did not quickly lose the remembrance of an injury. He always continued to speak with anger of the insolence and partiality of Page, and a short time before his death revenged it by a satire.

It is natural to inquire in what terms Mr Savage spoke of this fatal action, when the danger was over, and he was under no necessity of using any art to set his conduct in the fairest light. He was not willing to dwell upon it; and, if he transiently mentioned it, appeared neither to consider himself as a murderer, nor as a man wholly free from the guilt of blood. How much and how long he regretted it appeared in a poem which he published many years afterwards. On occasion of a copy of verses, in which the failings of good men were recounted, and in which the author had endeavoured to illustrate his position that 'the best may sometimes deviate from virtue,' by an instance of murder committed by Savage in the heat of wine, Savage remarked, that it was no very just representation of a good man to suppose him liable to drunkenness and disposed in his riots to cut throats.

He was now indeed at liberty, but was, as before, without any other support than accidental favours and uncertain patronage afforded him; sources by which he was sometimes very liberally supplied, and which at other times were suddenly stopped; so that he spent his life between want and plenty; or, what was yet worse, between beggary and extravagance; for as whatever he received was the gift of chance, which might as well favour him at one time as another, he was tempted to squander what he had because he always hoped to be immediately supplied.

Another cause of his profusion was the absurd kindness of his friends, who at once rewarded and enjoyed his abilities, by treating him at taverns, and habituating him to pleasures which he could not afford to enjoy, and which he was not able to deny himself, though he purchased the luxury of a single night by the anguish of cold and hunger for a week.

The experience of these inconveniencies determined him to endeavour after some settled income, which, having long found submission and entreaties fruitless, he attempted to extort from his mother by rougher methods. He had now, as he acknowledged, lost that tenderness for her, which the whole series of her cruelty had not been able wholly to repress, till he found, by the efforts which she made for his destruction, that she was not content with refusing to assist him, and being neutral in his struggles with poverty, but was as ready to snatch every opportunity of adding to his misfortunes; and that she was to be considered as an enemy implacably malicious, whom nothing but his blood could satisfy. He, therefore, threatened to harass her with lampoons, and to publish a copious narrative of her conduct, unless she consented to purchase an exemption from infamy, by allowing him a pension.

This expedient proved successful. Whether shame still survived, though virtue was extinct, or whether her relations had more delicacy than herself, and imagined that some of the darts which satire might point at her would glance upon them; Lord Tyrconnel, whatever were his motives, upon his promise to lay aside his design of exposing the cruelty of his mother, received him into his family, treated him as his equal, and engaged to allow him a pension of two hundred pounds a year.

This was the golden part of Mr Savage's life; and, for some time, he had no reason to complain of fortune; his appearance was splendid, his expenses large, and his acquaintance extensive. He was courted by all who endeavoured to be thought men of genius, and caressed by all who valued themselves upon a refined taste. To admire Mr Savage was a proof of discernment; and to be acquainted with him, was a title to poetical reputation. His presence was sufficient to make any place of publick entertainment popular; and his approbation and example constituted the fashion. So powerful is genius when it is invested with the glitter of affluence! Men willingly pay to fortune that regard which they owe to merit, and are pleased when they have an opportunity at once of gratifying their vanity, and practising their duty.

This interval of prosperity furnished him with opportunities of enlarging his knowledge of human nature by contemplating life from its highest gradations to its lowest; and, had he afterwards applied to dramatick poetry, he would perhaps not have had many superiours; for, as he never suffered any scene to pass before his eyes without notice, he had treasured in his mind all the different combinations of passions, and the innumerable mixtures of vice and virtue, which distinguish one character from another; and, as his conception was strong, his expressions were clear; he easily received impressions from objects, and very forcibly transmitted them to others.

Of his exact observations on human life he has left a proof, which would do honour to the greatest names, in a small pamphlet called the *Author to be Let*, where he introduces Iscariot Hackney, a prostitute scribbler, giving an account of his birth, his education, his disposition and morals, habits of life, and maxims of conduct. In the introduction are related many secret histories of the petty writers of that time, but sometimes mixed with ungenerous reflections on their birth, their circumstances, or those of their relations; nor can it be denied that some passages are such as Iscariot Hackney might himself have produced.

He was accused, likewise, of living in an appearance of friendship with some whom he satirized, and of making use of the confidence which he gained by a seeming kindness, to discover failings and expose them: it must be confessed, that Mr Savage's esteem was no very certain possession, and that he would lampoon at one time those whom he had praised at another.

It may be alleged that the same man may change his principles; and that he, who was once deservedly commended, may be afterwards satirized with equal justice; or that the poet was dazzled with the appearance of virtue, and found the man whom he had celebrated, when he had an opportunity of examining him more narrowly, unworthy of the panegyrick which he had too hastily bestowed; and that as a false satire ought to be recanted, for the sake of him whose reputation may be injured, false praise ought likewise to be obviated, lest the distinction between vice and virtue should be lost, lest a bad man should be trusted upon the credit of his encomiast, or lest others should endeavour to obtain the like praises by the same means.

But though these excuses may be often plausible, and sometimes just, they are very seldom satisfactory to mankind; and the writer who is not constant to his subject quickly sinks into contempt, his satire loses its force, and his panegyrick its value; and he is only considered at one time as a flatterer, and as a calumniator at another.

To avoid these imputations, it is only necessary to follow the rules of virtue, and to preserve an unvaried regard to truth. For though it is undoubtedly possible that a man, however cautious, may be sometimes deceived by an artful appearance of virtue, or by false evidences of guilt, such errours will not be frequent; and it will be allowed that the name of an author would never have been made contemptible, had no man ever said what he did not think, or misled others but when he was himself deceived.

The *Author to be Let* was first published in a single pamphlet, and afterwards inserted in a collection of pieces relating to the *Dunciad*, which were addressed by Mr Savage to the Earl of Middlesex, in a dedication which he was prevailed upon to sign, though he did not write it, and in which there are some positions, that the true author would, perhaps, not have published under his own name, and on which Mr Savage afterwards reflected with no great satisfaction; the enumeration of the bad effects of the uncontrouled freedom of the press, and the assertion that the 'liberties taken by the writers of journals with their superiours were exorbitant and unjustifiable,' very ill became men, who have themselves not always shown the exactest regard to the laws of subordination in their writings, and who have often satirized those that at least thought themselves their superiours, as they were eminent for their hereditary rank, and employed in the highest offices of the kingdom. But this is only an instance of that partiality which almost every man indulges with regard to himself: the liberty of the press is a blessing when we are inclined to write against others, and a calamity when we find ourselves overborne by the multitude of our assailants; as the power of the crown is always thought too great by those who suffer by its influence, and too little by those in whose favour it is exerted; and a standing army is generally accounted necessary by those who command, and dangerous and oppressive by those who support it.

Mr Savage was, likewise, very far from believing that the letters annexed to each species of bad poets in the *Bathos* were, as he was directed to assert, 'set down at random;' for when he was charged by one of his friends with putting his name to such an improbability, he had no other answer to make than that 'he did not think of it;' and his friend had too much tenderness to reply that next to the crime of writing contrary to what he thought, was that of writing without thinking.

After having remarked what is false in this dedication, it is proper that I observe the impartiality which I recommend by declaring what Savage asserted; that the account of the circumstances which attended the publication of the *Dunciad*, however strange and improbable, was exactly true.

The publication of this piece, at this time, raised Mr Savage a great number of enemies among those that were attacked by Mr Pope, with whom he was considered as a kind of confederate, and whom he was suspected of supplying with private intelligence and secret incidents: so that the ignominy of an informer was added to the terrour of a satirist.

That he was not altogether free from literary hypocrisy, and that he sometimes spoke one thing and wrote another, cannot be denied; because he himself confessed, that, when he lived in great familiarity with Dennis, he wrote an epigram against him.

Mr Savage, however, set all the malice of all the pygmy writers at defiance, and thought the friendship of Mr Pope cheaply purchased by being exposed to their censure and their hatred; nor had he any reason to repent of the preference, for he found Mr Pope a steady and unalienable friend almost to the end of his life.

About this time, notwithstanding his avowed neutrality with regard to party, he published a panegyrick on Sir Robert Walpole, for which he was rewarded by him with twenty guineas, a sum not very large, if either the excellence of the performance, or the affluence of the patron, be considered; but greater than he afterwards obtained from a person of yet higher rank, and more desirous in appearance of being distinguished as a patron of literature.

As he was very far from approving the conduct of Sir Robert Walpole, and in conversation mentioned him sometimes with acrimony, and generally with contempt; as he was one of those who were always zealous in their assertions of the justice of the late opposition, jealous of the rights of the people, and alarmed by the long-continued triumph of the court; it was natural to ask him what could induce him to employ his poetry in praise of that man, who was, in his opinion, an enemy to liberty, and an oppressor of his country? He alleged, that he was then dependent upon the Lord Tyrconnel, who was an implicit follower of the ministry, and that, being enjoined by him, not without menaces, to write in praise of his leader, he had not resolution sufficient to sacrifice the pleasure of affluence to that of integrity.

On this, and on many other occasions, he was ready to lament the misery of living at the tables of other men, which was his fate from the beginning to the end of his life; for I know not whether he ever had for three months together a settled habitation, in which he could claim a right of residence.

To this unhappy state it is just to impute much of the inconstancy of his conduct; for though a readiness to comply with the inclination of others was no part of his natural character, yet he was sometimes obliged to relax his obstinacy, and submit his own judgment, and even his virtue, to the government of those by whom he was supported: so that, if his miseries were sometimes the consequences of his faults, he ought not yet to be wholly excluded from compassion, because his faults were very often the effects of his misfortunes.

In this gay period of his life, while he was surrounded by affluence and pleasure, he published the *Wanderer*, a moral poem, of which the design is comprised in these lines:

> I fly all publick care, all venal strife,
> To try the still, compar'd with active life;
> To prove, by these, the sons of men may owe
> The fruits of bliss to bursting clouds of woe;
> That e'en calamity, by thought refin'd,
> Inspirits and adorns the thinking mind.

And more distinctly in the following passage:

> By woe, the soul to daring action swells;
> By woe, in plaintless patience it excels:
> From patience, prudent clear experience springs,
> And traces knowledge through the course of things!
> Thence hope is form'd, thence fortitude, success,
> Renown—whate'er men covet and caress.

This performance was always considered by himself as his masterpiece; and Mr Pope, when he asked his opinion of it, told him, that he read it once over, and was not displeased with it; that it gave him more pleasure at the second perusal, and delighted him still more at the third.

It has been generally objected to the *Wanderer*, that the disposition of the parts is irregular; that the design is obscure and the plan perplexed; that the images, however beautiful, succeed each other without order; and that the whole performance is not so much a regular fabrick, as a heap of shining materials thrown together by accident, which strikes rather with the solemn magnificence of a stupendous ruin, than the elegant grandeur of a finished pile.

This criticism is universal, and therefore it is reasonable to believe it at least in a great degree just; but Mr Savage was always of a contrary opinion, and thought his drift could only be missed by negligence or stupidity, and that the whole plan was regular, and the parts distinct.

It was never denied to abound with strong representations of nature, and just observations upon life; and it may easily be observed, that most of his pictures have an evident tendency to illustrate his first great position, 'that good is the consequence of evil.' The sun that burns up the mountains, fructifies the vales: the deluge that rushes down the broken rocks, with dreadful impetuosity, is separated into purling brooks; and the rage of the hurricane purifies the air.

Even in this poem he has not been able to forbear one touch upon the cruelty of his mother, which, though remarkably delicate and tender, is a proof how deep an impression it had upon his mind.

This must be at least acknowledged, which ought to be thought equivalent to many other excellencies, that this poem can promote no other purposes than those of virtue, and that it is written with a very strong sense of the efficacy of religion.

But my province is rather to give the history of Mr Savage's performances than to display their beauties, or to obviate the criticisms which they have occasioned; and therefore I shall not dwell upon the particular passages which deserve applause; I shall neither show the excellence of his descriptions, nor expatiate on the terrifick portrait of Suicide, nor point out the artful touches, by which he has distinguished the intellectual features of the rebels, who suffer death in his last canto. It is, however, proper to observe, that Mr Savage always declared the characters wholly fictitious, and without the least allusion to any real persons or actions.

From a poem so diligently laboured, and so successfully finished, it might be reasonably expected that he should have gained considerable advantage; nor can it, without some degree of indignation and concern, be told that he sold the copy for ten guineas, of which he afterwards returned two, that the two last sheets of the work might be reprinted, of which he had, in his absence, intrusted the correction to a friend, who was too indolent to perform it with accuracy.

A superstitious regard to the correction of his sheets was one of Mr Savage's peculiarities: he often altered, revised, recurred to his first reading or punctuation, and again adopted the alteration; he was dubious and irresolute without end, as on a question of the last importance, and at last was seldom satisfied: the intrusion or omission of a comma was sufficient to discompose him, and he would lament an errour of a single letter as a heavy calamity. In one of his letters relating to an impression of some verses he remarks, that he had, with regard to the correction of the proof, 'a spell upon him;' and indeed the anxiety, with which he dwelt upon the minutest and most trifling niceties, deserved no other name than that of fascination.

That he sold so valuable a performance for so small a price, was not to be imputed either to necessity, by which the learned and ingenious are often obliged to submit to very hard conditions; or to avarice, by which the booksellers are frequently incited to oppress that genius by which they are supported; but to that intemperate desire of pleasure, and habitual slavery to his passions, which involved him in many perplexities. He happened, at that time, to be engaged in the pursuit of some trifling gratification, and, being without money for the present occasion, sold his poem to the first bidder, and, perhaps, for the first price that was proposed; and would, probably, have been content with less, if less had been offered him.

This poem was addressed to the Lord Tyrconnel, not only in the first lines, but in a formal dedication, filled with the highest strains of panegyrick, and the warmest professions of gratitude, but by no means remarkable for delicacy of connexion or elegance of style.

These praises, in a short time, he found himself inclined to retract, being discarded by the man on whom he had bestowed them, and whom he then immediately discovered not to have deserved them. Of this quarrel, which every day made more bitter, Lord Tyrconnel and Mr Savage assigned very different reasons, which might perhaps all in reality concur, though they were not all convenient to be alleged by either party. Lord Tyrconnel affirmed, that it was the constant practice of Mr Savage to enter a tavern with any company that proposed it, drink the most expensive wines with great profusion, and, when the reckoning was demanded, to be without money: if, as it often happened, his company were willing to defray his part, the affair ended without any ill consequences; but if they were refractory, and expected that the wine should be paid for by him that drank it, his method of composition was, to take them with him to his own apartment, assume the government of the house, and order the butler, in an imperious manner, to set the best wine in the cellar before his company, who often drank till they forgot the respect due to the house in which they were entertained, indulged themselves in the utmost extravagance of merriment, practised the most licentious frolicks, and committed all the outrages of drunkenness.

Nor was this the only charge which Lord Tyrconnel brought against him. Having given him a collection of valuable books, stamped with his own arms, he had the mortification to see them, in a short time, exposed to sale upon the stalls, it being usual with Mr Savage, when he wanted a small sum, to take his books to the pawnbroker.

Whoever was acquainted with Mr Savage easily credited both these accusations; for having been obliged, from his first entrance into the world, to subsist upon expedients, affluence was not able to exalt him above them; and so much was he delighted with wine and conversation, and so long had he been accustomed to live by chance, that he would, at any time, go to the tavern without scruple, and trust for the reckoning to the liberality of his company, and frequently of company to whom he was very little known. This conduct indeed very seldom drew upon him those inconveniencies that might be feared by any other person; for his conversation was so entertaining, and his address so pleasing, that few thought the pleasure which they received from him dearly purchased by paying for his wine. It was his peculiar happiness that he scarcely ever found a stranger whom he did not leave a friend; but it must likewise be added that he had not often a friend long, without obliging him to become a stranger.

Mr Savage, on the other hand, declared, that Lord Tyrconnel quarrelled with him, because he would not subtract from his own luxury and extravagance what he had promised to allow him, and that his resentment was only a plea for the violation of his promise. He asserted, that he had done nothing that ought to exclude him from that subsistence which he thought not so much a favour, as a debt, since it was offered him upon conditions which he had never broken; and that his only fault was that he could not be supported with nothing.

He acknowledged that Lord Tyrconnel often exhorted him to regulate his method of life, and not to spend all his nights in taverns, and that he appeared very desirous that he would pass those hours with him, which he so freely bestowed upon others. This demand Mr Savage considered as a censure of his conduct, which he could never patiently bear, and which, in the latter and cooler part of his life, was so offensive to him that he declared it as his resolution, 'to spurn that friend who should presume to dictate to him;' and it is not likely that, in his earlier years, he received admonitions with more calmness.

He was, likewise, inclined to resent such expectations, as tending to infringe his liberty, of which he was very jealous, when it was necessary to the gratification of his passions; and declared, that the request was still more unreasonable, as the company to which he was to have been confined was insupportably disagreeable. This assertion affords another instance of that inconsistency of his writings with his conversation, which was so often to be observed. He forgot how lavishly he had, in his dedication to the *Wanderer*, extolled the delicacy and penetration, the humanity and generosity, the candour and politeness of the man, whom, when he no longer loved him, he declared to be a wretch without understanding, without good-nature, and without justice; of whose name he thought himself obliged to leave no trace in any future edition of his writings; and, accordingly, blotted it out of that copy of the *Wanderer* which was in his hands.

During his continuance with the Lord Tyrconnel, he wrote the *Triumph of Health and Mirth*, on the recovery of Lady Tyrconnel from a languishing illness. This performance is remarkable, not only for the gaiety of the ideas and the melody of the numbers, but for the agreeable fiction upon which it is formed. Mirth, overwhelmed with sorrow for the sickness of her favourite, takes a flight in quest of her sister Health, whom she finds reclined upon the brow of a lofty mountain, amidst the fragrance of perpetual spring, with the breezes of the morning sporting about her. Being solicited by her sister Mirth, she readily promises her assistance, flies away in a cloud, and impregnates the waters of Bath with new virtues, by which the sickness of Belinda is relieved.

As the reputation of his abilities, the particular circumstances of his birth and life, the splendour of his appearance, and the distinction which was, for some time, paid him by Lord Tyrconnel, entitled him to familiarity with persons of higher rank than those to whose conversation he had been before admitted; he did not fail to gratify that curiosity, which induced him to take a nearer view of those whom their birth, their employments, or their fortunes, necessarily place at a distance from the greatest part of mankind, and to examine whether their merit was magnified or diminished by the medium through which it was contemplated; whether the splendour with which they dazzled their admirers was inherent in themselves, or only reflected on them by the objects that surrounded them; and whether great men were selected for high stations, or high stations made great men.

For this purpose he took all opportunities of conversing familiarly with those who were most conspicuous at that time for their power or their influence; he watched their looser moments, and examined their domestick behaviour, with that acuteness which nature had given him, and which the uncommon variety of his life had contributed to increase, and that inquisitiveness which must always be produced in a vigorous mind, by an absolute freedom from all pressing or domestick engagements.

His discernment was quick, and therefore he soon found in

every person, and in every affair, something that deserved attention; he was supported by others, without any care for himself, and was therefore at leisure to pursue his observations.

More circumstances to constitute a critick on human life could not easily concur; nor indeed could any man who assumed from accidental advantages more praise than he could justly claim from his real merit admit an acquaintance more dangerous than that of Savage; of whom likewise it must be confessed that abilities really exalted above the common level, or virtue refined from passion, or proof against corruption, could not easily find an abler judge, or a warmer advocate.

What was the result of Mr Savage's inquiry, though he was not much accustomed to conceal his discoveries, it may not be entirely safe to relate, because the persons whose characters he criticised are powerful; and power and resentment are seldom strangers; nor would it, perhaps, be wholly just, because what he asserted in conversation might, though true in general, be heightened by some momentary ardour of imagination, and, as it can be delivered only from memory, may be imperfectly represented; so that the picture at first aggravated, and then unskilfully copied, may be justly suspected to retain no great resemblance of the original.

It may however be observed that he did not appear to have formed very elevated ideas of those to whom the administration of affairs, or the conduct of parties, has been entrusted; who have been considered as the advocates of the Crown, or the guardians of the people; and who have obtained the most implicit confidence and the loudest applauses. Of one particular person, who has been at one time so popular as to be generally esteemed, and at another so formidable as to be universally detested, he observed, that his acquisitions had been small, or that his capacity was narrow, and that the whole range of his mind was from obscenity to politicks, and from politicks to obscenity.

But the opportunity of indulging his speculations on great characters was now at an end. He was banished from the table of Lord Tyrconnel, and turned again adrift upon the world, without prospect of finding quickly any other harbour. As prudence was not one of the virtues by which he was distinguished, he had made no provision against a misfortune like this. And though it is not to be imagined but that the separation must, for some time, have been preceded by coldness, peevishness, or neglect, though it was undoubtedly the consequence of accumulated provocations on both sides; yet every one that knew Savage will readily believe, that to him it was sudden as a stroke of thunder; that, though he might have transiently suspected it, he had never suffered any thought so unpleasing to sink into his mind, but that he had driven it away by amusements, or dreams of future felicity and affluence, and had never taken any measures by which he might prevent a precipitation from plenty to indigence.

This quarrel and separation, and the difficulties to which Mr Savage was exposed by them, were soon known both to his friends and enemies; nor was it long before he perceived, from the behaviour of both, how much is added to the lustre of genius by the ornaments of wealth.

His condition did not appear to excite much compassion; for he had not always been careful to use the advantages he enjoyed with that moderation which ought to have been with more than usual caution preserved by him, who knew, if he had reflected, that he was only a dependant on the bounty of another, whom he could expect to support him no longer than he endeavoured to preserve his favour by complying with his inclinations, and whom he, nevertheless, set at defiance, and was continually irritating by negligence or encroachments.

Examples need not be sought at any great distance to prove that superiority of fortune has a natural tendency to kindle pride, and that pride seldom fails to exert itself in contempt and insult; and if this is often the effect of hereditary wealth, and of honours enjoyed only by the merit of others, it is some extenuation of any indecent triumphs to which this unhappy man may have been betrayed that his prosperity was heightened by the force of novelty, and made more intoxicating by a sense of the misery in which he had so long languished, and perhaps of the insults which he had formerly borne, and which he might now think himself entitled to revenge. It is too common for those who have unjustly suffered pain, to inflict it likewise in their turn, with the same injustice, and to imagine that they have a right to treat others as they have themselves been treated.

That Mr Savage was too much elevated by any good fortune, is generally known; and some passages of his introduction to the *Author to be Let*, sufficiently show, that he did not wholly refrain from such satire, as he afterwards thought very unjust when he was exposed to it himself; for, when he was afterwards ridiculed in the character of a distressed poet, he very easily discovered that distress was not a proper subject for merriment, or topick of invective. He was then able to discern, that if misery be the effect of virtue, it ought to be reverenced; if of ill fortune, to be pitied; and if of vice, not to be insulted, because it is, perhaps, itself a punishment adequate to the crime by which it was produced. And the humanity of that man can deserve no panegyrick, who is capable of reproaching a criminal in the hands of the executioner.

But these reflections, though they readily occurred to him in the first and last parts of his life, were, I am afraid, for a long time forgotten; at least they were, like many other maxims, treasured up in his mind rather for show than use, and operated very little upon his conduct, however elegantly he might sometimes explain, or however forcibly he might inculcate them.

His degradation therefore from the condition which he had enjoyed with such wanton thoughtlessness, was considered by many as an occasion of triumph. Those who had before paid their court to him without success, soon returned the contempt which they had suffered; and they who had received favours from him, for of such favours as he could bestow he was very liberal, did not always remember them. So much more certain are the effects of resentment than of gratitude: it is not only to many more pleasing to recollect those faults which place others below them than those virtues by which they are themselves comparatively depressed; but it is likewise more easy to neglect than to recompense; and though there are few who will practise a laborious virtue, there will never be wanting multitudes that will indulge an easy vice.

Savage however was very little disturbed at the marks of contempt which his ill fortune brought upon him, from those whom he never esteemed, and with whom he never considered himself as levelled by any calamities; and though it was not without some uneasiness that he saw some, whose friendship he valued, change their behaviour; he yet observed their coldness without much emotion, considered them as the slaves of fortune and the worshippers of prosperity, and was more inclined to despise them than to lament himself.

It does not appear that, after this return of his wants, he found mankind equally favourable to him, as at his first appearance in the world. His story, though in reality not less melancholy, was less affecting, because it was no longer new; it therefore procured him no new friends; and those that had formerly relieved him, thought they might now consign him to others. He was now likewise considered by many rather as criminal, than as unhappy; for the friends of Lord Tyrconnel, and of his mother, were sufficiently industrious to publish his weaknesses, which were indeed very numerous; and nothing was forgotten that might make him either hateful or ridiculous.

It cannot but be imagined that such representations of his faults must make great numbers less sensible of his distress; many who had only an opportunity to hear one part made no scruple to propagate the account which they received; many assisted their circulation from malice or revenge; and perhaps many pretended to credit them that they might, with a better grace, withdraw their regard, or withhold their assistance.

Savage however was not one of those who suffered himself to be injured without resistance, nor was less diligent in exposing the faults of Lord Tyrconnel; over whom he obtained at least this advantage, that he drove him first to the practice of outrage and violence; for he was so much provoked by the wit and virulence of Savage that he came, with a number of attendants that did no honour to his courage, to beat him at a coffee-house. But it happened that he had left the place a few minutes; and his lordship had without danger the pleasure of boasting how he would have treated him. Mr Savage went next day to repay his visit at his own house; but was prevailed on by his domesticks to retire without insisting upon seeing him.

Lord Tyrconnel was accused by Mr Savage of some actions, which scarcely any provocations will be thought sufficient to justify; such as seizing what he had in his lodgings, and other instances of wanton cruelty, by which he increased the distress of Savage, without any advantage to himself.

These mutual accusations were retorted on both sides, for many years, with the utmost degree of virulence and rage; and time seemed rather to augment than diminish their resentment. That the anger of Mr Savage should be kept alive is not strange, because he felt every day the consequences of the quarrel; but it might reasonably have been hoped that Lord Tyrconnel might have relented, and at length have forgot those provocations, which however they might have once inflamed him had not, in reality, much hurt him.

The spirit of Mr Savage indeed never suffered him to solicit a reconciliation; he returned reproach for reproach, and insult for insult; his superiority of wit supplied the disadvantages of his fortune, and enabled him to form a party, and prejudice great numbers in his favour.

But, though this might be some gratification of his vanity, it afforded very little relief to his necessities; and he was very frequently reduced to uncommon hardships, of which however he never made any mean or importunate complaints, being formed rather to bear misery with fortitude, than enjoy prosperity with moderation.

He now thought himself again at liberty to expose the cruelty of his mother; and therefore I believe, about this time, published the *Bastard*, a poem remarkable for the vivacious sallies of thought in the beginning, where he makes a pompous enumeration of the imaginary advantages of base birth; and the pathetick sentiments at the end, where he recounts the real calamities which he suffered by the crime of his parents.

The vigour and spirit of the verses, the peculiar circumstances of the author, the novelty of the subject, and the notoriety of

the story to which the allusions are made, procured this performance a very favourable reception; great numbers were immediately dispersed, and editions were multiplied with unusual
rapidity.

One circumstance attended the publication, which Savage
used to relate with great satisfaction: his mother, to whom the
poem was with 'due reverence' inscribed, happened then to be
at Bath, where she could not conveniently retire from censure,
or conceal herself from observation; and no sooner did the reputation of the poem begin to spread, than she heard it repeated
in all places of concourse; nor could she enter the assembly-
rooms, or cross the walks, without being saluted with some lines
from the *Bastard*.

This was, perhaps, the first time that she ever discovered a
sense of shame, and on this occasion the power of wit was very
conspicuous; the wretch who had, without scruple, proclaimed
herself an adulteress, and who had first endeavoured to starve
her son, then to transport him, and afterwards to hang him, was
not able to bear the representation of her own conduct; but fled
from reproach, though she felt no pain from guilt, and left Bath
with the utmost haste, to shelter herself among the crowds of
London.

Thus Savage had the satisfaction of finding that, though he
could not reform his mother, he could punish her, and that he
did not always suffer alone.

The pleasure which he received from this increase of his
poetical reputation was sufficient, for some time, to overbalance
the miseries of want, which this performance did not much
alleviate; for it was sold for a very trivial sum to a bookseller,
who, though the success was so uncommon that five impressions
were sold, of which many were, undoubtedly, very numerous,

had not generosity sufficient to admit the unhappy writer to any part of the profit.

The sale of this poem was always mentioned by Savage with the utmost elevation of heart, and referred to by him as an incontestable proof of a general acknowledgment of his abilities. It was indeed the only production of which he could justly boast a general reception.

But though he did not lose the opportunity which success gave him of setting a high rate on his abilities, but paid due deference to the suffrages of mankind when they were given in his favour, he did not suffer his esteem of himself to depend upon others, nor found any thing sacred in the voice of the people, when they were inclined to censure him; he then readily showed the folly of expecting that the publick should judge right, observed how slowly poetical merit had often forced its way into the world; he contented himself with the applause of men of judgment, and was somewhat disposed to exclude all those from the character of men of judgment who did not applaud him.

But he was at other times more favourable to mankind than to think them blind to the beauties of his works, and imputed the slowness of their sale to other causes; either they were published at a time when the town was empty, or when the attention of the publick was engrossed by some struggle in the Parliament, or some other object of general concern; or they were, by the neglect of the publisher, not diligently dispersed, or by his avarice not advertised with sufficient frequency. Address, or industry, or liberality, was always wanting; and the blame was laid rather on any person than the author.

By arts like these, arts which every man practises in some degree, and to which too much of the little tranquillity of life is to be ascribed, Savage was always able to live at peace with himself. Had he indeed only made use of these expedients to alleviate the loss or want of fortune or reputation, or any other advantages which it is not in man's power to bestow upon himself, they might have been justly mentioned as instances of a philosophical mind, and very properly proposed to the imitation of multitudes, who, for want of diverting their imaginations with the same dexterity, languish under afflictions which might be easily removed.

It were, doubtless, to be wished that truth and reason were universally prevalent; that every thing were esteemed according to its real value; and that men would secure themselves from being disappointed in their endeavours after happiness, by placing it only in virtue, which is always to be obtained; but, if adventitious and foreign pleasures must be pursued, it would be perhaps of some benefit, since that pursuit must frequently be fruitless, if the practice of Savage could be taught, that folly might be an antidote to folly, and one fallacy be obviated by another.

But the danger of this pleasing intoxication must not be concealed; nor indeed can any one, after having observed the life of Savage, need to be cautioned against it. By imputing none of his miseries to himself, he continued to act upon the same principles, and to follow the same path; was never made wiser by his sufferings, nor preserved by one misfortune from falling into another. He proceeded, throughout his life, to tread the same steps on the same circle; always applauding his past conduct or at least forgetting it to amuse himself with phantoms of happiness, which were dancing before him; and willingly turned his eyes from the light of reason, when it would have discovered the illusion, and shown him, what he never wished to see, his real state.

He is even accused, after having lulled his imagination with those ideal opiates, of having tried the same experiment upon his conscience; and, having accustomed himself to impute all deviations from the right to foreign causes, it is certain that he was, upon every occasion, too easily reconciled to himself, and that he appeared very little to regret those practices which had impaired his reputation. The reigning error of his life was, that he mistook the love for the practice of virtue, and was indeed not so much a good man as the friend of goodness.

This, at least, must be allowed him, that he always preserved a strong sense of the dignity, the beauty, and the necessity of virtue; and that he never contributed deliberately to spread corruption amongst mankind. His actions, which were generally precipitate, were often blameable; but his writings, being the productions of study, uniformly tended to the exaltation of the mind, and the propagation of morality and piety.

These writings may improve mankind, when his failings shall be forgotten; and, therefore, he must be considered, upon the whole, as a benefactor to the world; nor can his personal example do any hurt, since whoever hears of his faults will hear of the miseries which they brought upon him, and which would deserve less pity, had not his condition been such as made his faults pardonable. He may be considered as a child exposed to all the temptations of indigence, at an age when resolution was not yet strengthened by conviction, nor virtue confirmed by habit; a circumstance which, in his *Bastard*, he laments in a very affecting manner:

> No mother's care
> Shielded my infant innocence with pray'r:
> No father's guardian hand my youth maintain'd,
> Call'd forth my virtues, or from vice restrain'd.

The *Bastard*, however it might provoke or mortify his mother, could not be expected to melt her to compassion, so that he was still under the same want of the necessaries of life; and he therefore exerted all the interest which his wit, or his birth, or his misfortunes, could procure, to obtain upon the death of Eusden the place of Poet Laureate, and prosecuted his application with so much diligence, that the king publickly declared it his intention to bestow it upon him; but such was the fate of Savage, that even the king, when he intended his advantage, was disappointed in his schemes; for the lord chamberlain, who has the disposal of the laurel, as one of the appendages of his office, either did not know the King's design, or did not approve it, or thought the nomination of the laureate an encroachment upon his rights, and therefore bestowed the laurel upon Colley Cibber.

Mr Savage, thus disappointed, took a resolution of applying to the Queen, that, having once given him life, she would enable him to support it, and therefore published a short poem on her birthday, to which he gave the odd title of Volunteer Laureate. The event of this essay he has himself related in the following letter, which he pre-fixed to the poem, when he afterwards reprinted it in the *Gentleman's Magazine*, from whence I have copied it entire, as this was one of the few attempts in which Mr Savage succeeded.

'MR URBAN,—In your magazine for February you published the last Volunteer Laureate, written on a very melancholy occasion, the death of the royal patroness of arts and literature in general, and of the author of that poem in particular; I now send you the first that Mr Savage wrote under that title. This gentleman, notwithstanding a very considerable interest, being, on the death of Mr Eusden, disappointed of the laureate's place,

wrote the before-mentioned poem; which was no sooner published, but the late queen sent to a bookseller for it. The author
had not at that time a friend either to get him introduced, or
his poem presented at court; yet such was the unspeakable goodness of that princess, that, notwithstanding this act of ceremony
was wanting, in a few days after publication, Mr Savage received
a bank bill of fifty pounds, and a gracious message from her
majesty, by the Lord North and Guildford, to this effect: 'That
her majesty was highly pleased with the verses; that she took
particularly kind his lines there relating to the king; that he had
permission to write annually on the same subject; and that he
should yearly receive the like present, till something better (which
was her majesty's intention) could be done for him.' After this,
he was permitted to present one of his annual poems to her
majesty, had the honour of kissing her hand, and met with the
most gracious reception.

'Yours, &c.'

Such was the performance, and such its reception; a reception,
which, though by no means unkind, was yet not in the highest
degree generous: to chain down the genius of a writer to an
annual panegyrick, showed in the Queen too much desire of
hearing her own praises, and a greater regard to herself than to
him on whom her bounty was conferred. It was a kind of avar-
icious generosity, by which flattery was rather purchased than
genius rewarded.

Mrs Oldfield had formerly given him the same allowance with
much more heroick intention: she had no other view than to
enable him to prosecute his studies, and to set himself above
the want of assistance, and was contented with doing good
without stipulating for encomiums.

Mr Savage, however, was not at liberty to make exceptions,
but was ravished with the favours which he had received, and

probably yet more with those which he was promised: he considered himself now as a favourite of the queen, and did not doubt but a few annual poems would establish him in some profitable employment.

He therefore assumed the title of Volunteer Laureate, not without some reprehensions from Cibber who informed him that the title of laureate was a mark of honour conferred by the king, from whom all honour is derived, and which therefore no man has a right to bestow upon himself; and added that he might with equal propriety style himself a volunteer lord or volunteer baronet. It cannot be denied that the remark was just; but Savage did not think any title, which was conferred upon Mr Cibber, so honourable as that the usurpation of it could be imputed to him as an instance of very exorbitant vanity, and, therefore, continued to write under the same title, and received every year the same reward.

He did not appear to consider these encomiums as tests of his abilities, or as any thing more than annual hints to the queen of her promise, or acts of ceremony, by the performance of which he was entitled to his pension, and therefore did not labour them with great diligence, or print more than fifty each year, except that for some of the last years he regularly inserted them in the *Gentleman's Magazine*, by which they were dispersed over the kingdom.

Of some of them he had himself so low an opinion, that he intended to omit them in the collection of poems, for which he printed proposals, and solicited subscriptions; nor can it seem strange, that, being confined to the same subject, he should be at some times indolent, and at others unsuccessful; that he should sometimes delay a disagreeable task till it was too late to perform it well; or that he should sometimes repeat the same sentiment on the same occasion, or at others be misled by an attempt after novelty to forced conceptions and far-fetched images.

He wrote indeed with a double intention, which supplied him with some variety; for his business was to praise the Queen for the favours which he had received, and to complain to her of the delay of those which she had promised: in some of his pieces therefore, gratitude is predominant, and in some discontent; in some he represents himself as happy in her patronage; and, in others, as disconsolate to find himself neglected.

Her promise, like other promises made to this unfortunate man, was never performed, though he took sufficient care that it should not be forgotten. The publication of his 'Volunteer Laureate' procured him no other reward than a regular remittance of fifty pounds.

He was not so depressed by his disappointments as to neglect any opportunity that was offered of advancing his interest. When the Princess Anne was married, he wrote a poem upon her departure, only, as he declared, 'because it was expected from him,' and he was not willing to bar his own prospects by any appearance of neglect.

He never mentioned any advantage gained by this poem, or any regard that was paid to it; and therefore it is likely that it was considered at court as an act of duty, to which he was obliged by his dependence, and which it was therefore not necessary to reward by any new favour: or perhaps the Queen really intended his advancement, and therefore thought it superfluous to lavish presents upon a man whom she intended to establish for life.

About this time not only his hopes were in danger of being frustrated, but his pension likewise of being obstructed, by an accidental calumny. The writer of the *Daily Courant*, a paper then published under the direction of the Ministry, charged him with a crime, which, though not very great in itself, would have been remarkably invidious in him, and might very justly have incensed the Queen against him. He was accused by name of influencing elections against the court, by appearing at the head of a Tory mob; nor did the accuser fail to aggravate his crime, by representing it as the effect of the most atrocious ingratitude, and a kind of rebellion against the queen, who had first preserved him from an infamous death, and afterwards distinguished him by her favour, and supported him by her charity. The charge, as it was open and confident, was likewise, by good fortune, very particular. The place of the transaction was mentioned, and the whole series of the rioter's conduct related. This exactness made Mr Savage's vindication easy; for he never had in his life seen the place which was declared to be the scene of his wickedness, nor ever had been present in any town when its representatives were chosen. This answer he therefore made haste to publish, with all the circumstances necessary to make it credible; and very reasonably demanded, that the accusation should be retracted in the same paper, that he might no longer suffer the imputation of sedition and ingratitude. This demand was likewise pressed by him in a private letter to the author of the paper, who, either trusting to the protection of those whose defence he had undertaken, or having entertained some personal malice against Mr Savage, or fearing lest, by retracting so confident an assertion, he should impair the credit of his paper, refused to give him that satisfaction.

Mr Savage therefore thought it necessary, to his own vindication, to prosecute him in the King's Bench; but as he did not find any ill effects from the accusation, having sufficiently cleared his innocence, he thought any further procedure would have the appearance of revenge; and, therefore, willingly dropped it.

He saw, soon afterwards, a process commenced in the same court against himself, on an information in which he was accused of writing and publishing an obscene pamphlet.

It was always Mr Savage's desire to be distinguished; and, when any controversy became popular, he never wanted some reason for engaging in it with great ardour, and appearing at the head of the party which he had chosen. As he was never celebrated for his prudence, he had no sooner taken his side, and informed himself of the chief topicks of the dispute, than he took all opportunities of asserting and propagating his principles, without much regard to his own interest, or any other visible design than that of drawing upon himself the attention of mankind.

The dispute between the Bishop of London and the Chancellor is well known to have been, for some time, the chief topick of political conversation; and therefore Mr Savage, in pursuance of his character, endeavoured to become conspicuous among the controvertists with which every coffee-house was filled on that occasion. He was an indefatigable opposer of all the claims of ecclesiastical power, though he did not know on what they were founded; and was, therefore, no friend to the Bishop of London. But he had another reason for appearing as a warm advocate for Dr Rundle; for he was the friend of Mr Foster and Mr Thomson, who were the friends of Mr Savage.

Thus remote was his interest in the question, which however as he imagined, concerned him so nearly, that it was not sufficient to harangue and dispute, but necessary likewise to write upon it.

He therefore engaged with great ardour in a new poem, called by him, the *Progress of a Divine*; in which he conducts a profligate priest, by all the gradations of wickedness, from a poor curacy in the country to the highest preferments of the church; and describes, with that humour which was natural to him, and that knowledge which was extended to all the diversities of human life, his behaviour in every station; and insinuates, that this priest, thus accomplished, found at last a patron in the Bishop of London.

When he was asked by one of his friends, on what pretence he could charge the bishop with such an action, he had no more to say than that he had only inverted the accusation; and that he thought it reasonable to believe, that he who obstructed the rise of a good man without reason, would, for bad reasons, promote the exaltation of a villain.

The clergy were universally provoked by this satire; and Savage, who, as was his constant practice, had set his name to his performance, was censured in the *Weekly Miscellany** with severity, which he did not seem inclined to forget.

---

* A short satire was, likewise, published in the same paper, in which were the following lines:

> For cruel murder doom'd to hempen death,
> Savage, by royal grace, prolong'd his breath.
> Well might you think he spent his future years
> In pray'r, and fasting, and repentant tears.
> —But, O vain hope! – the truly Savage cries,
> 'Priests, and their slavish doctrines, I despise.
> Shall I—
> Who, by free-thinking to free action fir'd,
> In midnight brawls a deathless name acquir'd,
> Now stoop to learn of ecclesiastic men?—
> No, arm'd with rhyme, at priests I'll take my aim,
> Though prudence bids me murder but their fame.'
> *Weekly Miscellany.*

An answer was published in the *Gentleman's Magazine*, written by an unknown hand, from which the following lines are selected:

But a return of invective was not thought a sufficient punishment. The Court of King's Bench was, therefore, moved against him; and he was obliged to return an answer to a charge of obscenity. It was urged in his defence, that obscenity was criminal when it was intended to promote the practice of vice; but that Mr Savage had only introduced obscene ideas, with the view of exposing them to detestation, and of amending the age, by showing the deformity of wickedness. This plea was admitted; and Sir Philip Yorke, who then presided in that court, dismissed the information with encomiums upon the purity and excellence of Mr Savage's writings. The prosecution, however, answered

---

> Transform'd by thoughtless rage, and midnight wine,
> From malice free, and push'd without design;
> In equal brawl if Savage lung'd a thrust,
> And brought the youth a victim to the dust;
> So strong the hand of accident appears,
> The royal hand from guilt and vengeance clears.
>   Instead of wasting 'all thy future years,
> Savage, in pray'r and vain repentant tears,'
> Exert thy pen to mend a vicious age,
> To curb the priest, and sink his high-church rage;
> To show what frauds the holy vestments hide,
> The nests of av'rice, lust, and pedant pride:
> Then change the scene, let merit brightly shine,
> And round the patriot twist the wreath divine;
> The heav'nly guide deliver down to fame;
> In well-tun'd lays transmit a Foster's name;
> Touch ev'ry passion with harmonious art,
> Exalt the genius, and correct the heart.
> Thus future times shall royal grace extol;
> Thus polish'd lines thy present fame enrol.
> ——But grant——
> ——Maliciously that Savage plung'd the steel,
> And made the youth its shining vengeance feel;
> My soul abhors the act, the man detests,
> But more the bigotry in priestly breasts.
> _Gentleman's Magazine_, May, 1735.

in some measure the purpose of those by whom it was set on foot; for Mr Savage was so far intimidated by it, that, when the edition of his poem was sold, he did not venture to reprint it; so that it was in a short time forgotten, or forgotten by all but those whom it offended.

It is said that some endeavours were used to incense the Queen against him: but he found advocates to obviate, at least, part of their effect; for, though he was never advanced, he still continued to receive his pension.

This poem drew more infamy upon him than any incident of his life; and, as his conduct cannot be vindicated, it is proper to secure his memory from reproach, by informing those whom he made his enemies, that he never intended to repeat the provocation; and that though whenever he thought he had any reason to complain of the clergy, he used to threaten them with a new edition of the *Progress of a Divine*, it was his calm and settled resolution to suppress it for ever.

He once intended to have made a better reparation for the folly or injustice with which he might be charged, by writing another poem, called the *Progress of a Freethinker*, whom he intended to lead through all the stages of vice and folly, to convert him from virtue to wickedness, and from religion to infidelity, by all the modish sophistry used for that purpose; and, at last, to dismiss him by his own hand into the other world.

That he did not execute this design is a real loss to mankind; for he was too well acquainted with all the scenes of debauchery to have failed in his representations of them, and too zealous for virtue not to have represented them in such a manner as should expose them either to ridicule or detestation.

But this plan was, like others, formed and laid aside, till the vigour of his imagination was spent, and the effervescence of invention had subsided; but soon gave way to some other design, which pleased by its novelty for awhile, and then was neglected like the former.

He was still in his usual exigencies, having no certain support but the pension allowed him by the Queen, which, though it might have kept an exact economist from want, was very far from being sufficient for Mr Savage, who had never been accustomed to dismiss any of his appetites without the gratification which they solicited, and whom nothing but want of money withheld from partaking of every pleasure that fell within his view.

His conduct, with regard to his pension, was very particular. No sooner had he changed the bill, than he vanished from the sight of all his acquaintances, and lay, for some time, out of the reach of all the inquiries that friendship or curiosity could make after him. At length he appeared again penniless as before, but never informed even those whom he seemed to regard most, where he had been; nor was his retreat ever discovered.

This was his constant practice during the whole time that he received the pension from the Queen: he regularly disappeared and returned. He, indeed, affirmed that he retired to study, and that the money supported him in solitude for many months; but his friends declared, that the short time in which it was spent sufficiently confuted his own account of his conduct.

His politeness and his wit still raised him friends, who were desirous of setting him at length free from that indigence by which he had been hitherto oppressed; and therefore solicited Sir Robert Walpole in his favour with so much earnestness, that they obtained a promise of the next place that should become vacant, not exceeding two hundred pounds a year. This promise was made with an uncommon declaration, 'that it was not the promise of a minister to a petitioner, but of a friend to his friend.'

Mr Savage now concluded himself set at ease for ever, and, as he observes in a poem written on that incident of his life, trusted and was trusted; but soon found that his confidence was ill-grounded, and this friendly promise was not inviolable. He spent a long time in solicitations, and, at last despaired and desisted.

He did not indeed deny, that he had given the minister some reason to believe that he should not strengthen his own interest by advancing him, for he had taken care to distinguish himself in coffee-houses as an advocate for the Ministry of the last years of Queen Anne, and was always ready to justify the conduct, and exalt the character of Lord Bolingbroke, whom he mentions with great regard in an *Epistle upon Authors*, which he wrote about that time, but was too wise to publish, and of which only some fragments have appeared, inserted by him in the magazine after his retirement.

To despair was not however the character of Savage; when one patronage failed, he had recourse to another. The prince was now extremely popular, and had very liberally rewarded the merit of some writers, whom Mr Savage did not think superiour to himself, and, therefore, he resolved to address a poem to him.

For this purpose he made choice of a subject which could regard only persons of the highest rank and greatest affluence, and which was therefore proper for a poem intended to procure the patronage of a prince; and, having retired for some time to Richmond, that he might prosecute his design in full tranquillity, without the temptations of pleasure, or the solicitations of creditors, by which his meditations were in equal danger of being disconcerted, he produced a poem on *Publick Spirit, with regard to Publick Works*.

The plan of this poem is very extensive, and comprises a multitude of topicks, each of which might furnish matter sufficient for a long performance, and of which some have already employed more eminent writers; but as he was, perhaps, not fully acquainted with the whole extent of his own design, and was writing to obtain a supply of wants too pressing to admit of long or accurate inquiries, he passes negligently over many publick works, which, even in his own opinion, deserved to be more elaborately treated.

But, though he may sometimes disappoint his reader by transient touches upon these subjects, which have often been considered, and, therefore, naturally raise expectations, he must be allowed amply to compensate his omissions, by expatiating, in the conclusion of his work, upon a kind of beneficence not yet celebrated by any eminent poet, though it now appears more susceptible of embellishments, more adapted to exalt the ideas, and affect the passions, than many of those which have hitherto been thought most worthy of the ornaments of verse. The settlement of colonies in uninhabited countries, the establishment of those in security, whose misfortunes have made their own country no longer pleasing or safe, the acquisition of property without injury to any, the appropriation of the waste and luxuriant bounties of nature, and the enjoyment of those gifts which heaven has scattered upon regions uncultivated and unoccupied, cannot be considered without giving rise to a great number of pleasing ideas, and bewildering the imagination in delightful prospects; and therefore whatever speculations they may produce in those who have confined themselves to political studies, naturally fixed the attention, and excited the applause, of a poet. The politician, when he considers men driven into other countries for shelter, and obliged to retire to forests and deserts, and pass their lives, and fix their posterity, in the remotest corners of the world, to avoid those hardships which they suffer or fear in their native place, may very properly inquire, why the legislature does not provide a remedy for these miseries, rather than encourage an escape from them. He may conclude that the flight of every honest man is a loss to the community; that those who are unhappy without guilt ought to be relieved; and the life, which is overburdened by accidental calamities, set at ease by the care of the publick; and that those, who have by misconduct forfeited their claim to favour, ought rather to be made useful to the society which they have injured, than driven from it. But the poet is employed in a more pleasing undertaking than that of proposing laws which, however just or expedient, will never be made; or endeavouring to reduce to rational schemes of government societies which were formed by chance, and are conducted by the private passions of those who preside in them. He guides the unhappy fugitive, from want and persecution, to plenty, quiet, and security, and seats him in scenes of peaceful solitude, and undisturbed repose.

Savage has not forgotten, amidst the pleasing sentiments which this prospect of retirement suggested to him, to censure those crimes which have been generally committed by the discoverers of new regions, and to expose the enormous wickedness of making war upon barbarous nations because they cannot resist, and of invading countries because they are fruitful; of extending navigation only to propagate vice, and of visiting distant lands only to lay them waste. He has asserted the natural equality of mankind, and endeavoured to suppress that pride which inclines men to imagine that right is the consequence of power.

His description of the various miseries which force men to

seek for refuge in distant countries, affords another instance of his proficiency in the important and extensive study of human life; and the tenderness with which he recounts them, another proof of his humanity and benevolence.

It is observable, that the close of this poem discovers a change which experience had made in Mr Savage's opinions. In a poem written by him in his youth, and published in his *Miscellanies*, he declares his contempt of the contracted views and narrow prospects of the middle state of life, and declares his resolution either to tower like the cedar, or be trampled like the shrub; but in this poem, though addressed to a prince, he mentions this state of life as comprising those who ought most to attract reward, those who merit most the confidence of power, and the familiarity of greatness; and, accidentally mentioning this passage to one of his friends, declared that, in his opinion, all the virtue of mankind was comprehended in that state.

In describing villas and gardens, he did not omit to condemn that absurd custom which prevails among the English, of permitting servants to receive money from strangers for the entertainment that they receive, and, therefore, inserted in his poem these lines:

> But what the flow'ring pride of gardens rare,
> However royal, or however fair:
> If gates, which to access should still give way,
> Ope but, like Peter's Paradise, for pay?
> If perquisited varlets frequent stand,
> And each new walk must a new tax demand?
> What foreign eye but with contempt surveys?
> What muse shall from oblivion snatch their praise?

But before the publication of his performance he recollected, that the Queen allowed her garden and cave at Richmond to be shown for money; and that she so openly countenanced the practice, that she had bestowed the privilege of showing them as a place of profit on a man, whose merit she valued herself upon rewarding, though she gave him only the liberty of disgracing his country.

He therefore thought, with more prudence than was often exerted by him, that the publication of these lines might be officiously represented as an insult upon the Queen, to whom he owed his life and his subsistence: and that the propriety of his observation would be no security against the censures which the unreasonableness of it might draw upon him; he, therefore, suppressed the passage in the first edition, but after the Queen's death thought the same caution no longer necessary, and restored it to the proper place.

The poem was, therefore, published without any political faults, and inscribed to the Prince: but Mr Savage, having no friend upon whom he could prevail to present it to him, had no other method of attracting his observation than the publication of frequent advertisements, and therefore received no reward from his patron, however generous on other occasions.

This disappointment he never mentioned without indignation, being, by some means or other, confident that the Prince was not ignorant of his address to him; and insinuated, that if any advances in popularity could have been made by distinguishing him, he had not written without notice, or without reward.

He was once inclined to have presented his poem in person, and sent to the printer for a copy with that design; but either his opinion changed, or his resolution deserted him, and he continued to resent neglect without attempting to force himself into regard.

Nor was the publick much more favourable than his patron;

for only seventy-two were sold, though the performance was much commended by some whose judgment in that kind of writing is generally allowed. But Savage easily reconciled himself to mankind, without imputing any defect to his work, by observing, that his poem was unluckily published two days after the prorogation of the Parliament, and, by consequence, at a time when all those who could be expected to regard it were in the hurry of preparing for their departure, or engaged in taking leave of others upon their dismission from publick affairs.

It must be however allowed, in justification of the publick, that this performance is not the most excellent of Mr Savage's works; and that, though it cannot be denied to contain many striking sentiments, majestick lines, and just observations, it is in general not sufficiently polished in the language, or enlivened in the imagery, or digested in the plan.

Thus his poem contributed nothing to the alleviation of his poverty, which was such as very few could have supported with equal patience; but to which, it must likewise be confessed, that few would have been exposed, who received punctually fifty pounds a year; a salary which, though by no means equal to the demands of vanity and luxury, is yet found sufficient to support families above want, and was, undoubtedly, more than the necessities of life require.

But no sooner had he received his pension, than he withdrew to his darling privacy, from which he returned, in a short time, to his former distress, and, for some part of the year, generally lived by chance, eating only when he was invited to the tables of his acquaintances, from which the meanness of his dress often excluded him, when the politeness and variety of his conversation would have been thought a sufficient recompense for his entertainment.

He lodged as much by accident as he dined, and passed the night sometimes in mean houses, which are set open at night to any casual wanderers, sometimes in cellars, among the riot and filth of the meanest and most profligate of the rabble; and sometimes, when he had not money to support even the expenses of these receptacles, walked about the streets till he was weary, and lay down in the summer upon a bulk, or in the winter, with his associates in poverty, among the ashes of a glass-house.

In this manner were passed those days and those nights which nature had enabled him to have employed in elevated specu-lations, useful studies, or pleasing conversation. On a bulk, in a cellar, or in a glass-house, among thieves and beggars, was to be found the author of the *Wanderer*; the man of exalted sentiments, extensive views, and curious observations; the man whose remarks on life might have assisted the statesman, whose ideas of virtue might have enlightened the moralist, whose eloquence might have influenced senates, and whose delicacy might have polished courts.

It cannot but be imagined that such necessities might some-times force him upon disreputable practices; and it is probable that these lines in the *Wanderer* were occasioned by his reflec-tions on his own conduct:

> Though misery leads to happiness, and truth,
> Unequal to the load, this languid youth,
> (O, let none censure, if, untried by grief,
> If, amidst woe, untempted by relief,)
> He stoop'd reluctant to low arts of shame,
> Which then, e'en then, he scorn'd and blush'd to name.

Whoever was acquainted with him was certain to be solicited for small sums, which the frequency of the request made in time considerable; and he was therefore quickly shunned by those who were become familiar enough to be trusted with his necessities; but his rambling manner of life, and constant appearance at houses of publick resort, always procured him a new succession of friends, whose kindness had not been exhausted by repeated requests; so that he was seldom absolutely without resources but had in his utmost exigencies this comfort that he always imagined himself sure of speedy relief.

It was observed, that he always asked favours of this kind without the least submission or apparent consciousness of dependence, and that he did not seem to look upon a compliance with his request as an obligation that deserved any extraordinary acknowledgments; but a refusal was resented by him as an affront, or complained of as an injury; nor did he readily reconcile himself to those who either denied to lend, or gave him afterwards any intimation that they expected to be repaid.

He was sometimes so far compassionated by those who knew both his merit and distresses that they received him into their families; but they soon discovered him to be a very incommodious inmate; for, being always accustomed to an irregular manner of life, he could not confine himself to any stated hours, or pay any regard to the rules of a family, but would prolong his conversation till midnight, without considering that business might require his friend's application in the morning; and, when he had persuaded himself to retire to bed, was not, without equal difficulty, called up to dinner; it was therefore impossible to pay him any distinction without the entire subversion of all economy, a kind of establishment which, wherever he went, he always appeared ambitious to overthrow.

It must therefore be acknowledged, in justification of mankind, that it was not always by the negligence or coldness of his friends that Savage was distressed, but because it was in reality very difficult to preserve him long in a state of ease. To supply him with money was a hopeless attempt; for no sooner did he see himself master of a sum sufficient to set him free from care for a day than he became profuse and luxurious. When once he had entered a tavern, or engaged in a scheme of pleasure, he never retired till want of money obliged him to some new expedient. If he was entertained in a family, nothing was any longer to be regarded there but amusements and jollity; wherever Savage entered, he immediately expected that order and business should fly before him, that all should thenceforward be left to hazard, and that no dull principle of domestick management should be opposed to his inclination, or intrude upon his gaiety.

His distresses, however afflictive, never dejected him; in his lowest state he wanted not spirit to assert the natural dignity of wit, and was always ready to repress that insolence which superiority of fortune incited, and to trample on that reputation which rose upon any other basis than that of merit: he never admitted any gross familiarities, or submitted to be treated otherwise than as an equal. Once, when he was without lodging, meat, or clothes, one of his friends, a man not indeed remarkable for moderation in his prosperity, left a message that he desired to see him about nine in the morning. Savage knew that his intention was to assist him; but was very much disgusted that he should presume to prescribe the hour of his attendance, and, I believe, refused to visit him, and rejected his kindness.

The same invincible temper, whether firmness or obstinacy, appeared in his conduct to the Lord Tyrconnel, from whom he very frequently demanded, that the allowance which was once paid him should be restored; but with whom he never appeared to entertain, for a moment, the thought of soliciting a reconciliation, and whom he treated, at once, with all the haughtiness of superiority, and all the bitterness of resentment. He wrote to him, not in a style of supplication or respect, but of reproach, menace, and contempt; and appeared determined, if he ever regained his allowance, to hold it only by the right of conquest.

As many more can discover that a man is richer than that he is wiser than themselves, superiority of understanding is not so readily acknowledged as that of fortune; nor is that haughtiness, which the consciousness of great abilities incites, borne with the same submission as the tyranny of affluence; and therefore Savage, by asserting his claim to deference and regard, and by treating those with contempt whom better fortune animated to rebel against him, did not fail to raise a great number of enemies in the different classes of mankind. Those who thought themselves raised above him by the advantages of riches, hated him, because they found no protection from the petulance of his wit. Those who were esteemed for their writings feared him as a critick, and maligned him as a rival, and almost all the smaller wits were his professed enemies.

Among these Mr Miller so far indulged his resentment as to introduce him in a farce, and direct him to be personated on the stage, in a dress like that which he then wore; a mean insult, which only insinuated that Savage had but one coat, and which was therefore despised by him rather than resented: for, though he wrote a lampoon against Miller, he never printed it; and as no other person ought to prosecute that revenge from which the person who was injured desisted, I shall not preserve what Mr Savage suppressed; of which the publication would indeed have been a punishment too severe for so impotent an assault.

The great hardships of poverty were to Savage not the want of lodging or of food, but the neglect and contempt which it drew upon him. He complained that, as his affairs grew desperate, he found his reputation for capacity visibly decline; that his opinion in questions of criticism was no longer regarded, when his coat was out of fashion; and that those who, in the interval of his prosperity, were always encouraging him to great undertakings, by encomiums on his genius and assurances of success, now received any mention of his designs with coldness, thought that the subjects on which he proposed to write were very difficult, and were ready to inform him, that the event of a poem was uncertain, that an author ought to employ much time in the consideration of his plan, and not presume to sit down to write in confidence of a few cursory ideas, and a superficial knowledge; difficulties were started on all sides, and he was no longer qualified for any performance but the Volunteer Laureate.

Yet even this kind of contempt never depressed him; for he always preserved a steady confidence in his own capacity, and believed nothing above his reach, which he should at any time earnestly endeavour to attain. He formed schemes of the same kind with regard to knowledge and to fortune, and flattered himself with advances to be made in science, as with riches, to be enjoyed in some distant period of his life. For the acquisition of knowledge he was indeed far better qualified than for that of riches; for he was naturally inquisitive, and desirous of the conversation of those from whom any information was to be obtained, but by no means solicitous to improve those opportunities that were sometimes offered of raising his fortune; and he was remarkably retentive of his ideas, which, when once he was in possession of them, rarely forsook him; a quality which could never be communicated to his money.

While he was thus wearing out his life in expectation that the queen would some time recollect her promise, he had recourse to the usual practice of writers, and published proposals for printing his works by subscription, to which he was encouraged by the success of many who had not a better right to the favour of the publick; but, whatever was the reason, he did not find the world equally inclined to favour him; and he observed, with some discontent, that though he offered his works at half-a-guinea, he was able to procure but a small number in comparison with those who subscribed twice as much to Duck.

Nor was it without indignation that he saw his proposals neglected by the Queen, who patronised Mr Duck's with uncommon ardour, and incited a competition among those who attended the court, who should most promote his interest, and who should first offer a subscription. This was a distinction to which Mr Savage made no scruple of asserting, that his birth, his misfortunes, and his genius, gave him a fairer title, than could be pleaded by him on whom it was conferred.

Savage's applications were however not universally unsuccessful; for some of the nobility countenanced his design, encouraged his proposals, and subscribed with great liberality. He related of the Duke of Chandos particularly, that, upon receiving his proposals, he sent him ten guineas.

But the money which his subscriptions afforded him was not less volatile than that which he received from his other schemes; whenever a subscription was paid him, he went to a tavern; and, as money so collected is necessarily received in small sums, he never was able to send his poems to the press, but, for many years, continued his solicitation, and squandered whatever he obtained.

The project of printing his works was frequently revived; and, as his proposals grew obsolete, new ones were printed with fresher dates. To form schemes for the publication, was one of his favourite amusements; nor was he ever more at ease than when, with any friend who readily fell in with his schemes, he was adjusting the print, forming the advertisements, and regulating the dispersion of his new edition, which he really intended, some time, to publish; and which, as long experience had shown him the impossibility of printing the volume together, he at last determined to divide into weekly or monthly numbers, that the profits of the first might supply the expenses of the next.

Thus he spent his time in mean expedients and tormenting suspense, living, for the greatest part, in the fear of prosecutions from his creditors, and, consequently, skulking in obscure parts of the town, of which he was no stranger to the remotest corners. But, wherever he came, his address secured him friends, whom his necessities soon alienated; so that he had perhaps a more numerous acquaintance than any man ever before attained, there being scarcely any person eminent on any account to whom he was not known, or whose character he was not, in some degree, able to delineate.

To the acquisition of this extensive acquaintance every circumstance of his life contributed. He excelled in the arts of conversation, and therefore willingly practised them. He had seldom any home, or even a lodging, in which he could be private; and therefore was driven into publick-houses for the common conveniencies of life and supports of nature. He was always ready to comply with every invitation, having no employment to withhold him, and often no money to provide for himself; and, by dining with one company, he never failed of obtaining an introduction into another.

Thus dissipated was his life, and thus casual his subsistence; yet did not the distraction of his views hinder him from reflection, nor the uncertainty of his condition depress his gaiety. When he had wandered about without any fortunate adventure by which he was led into a tavern, he sometimes retired into the fields, and was able to employ his mind in study, or amuse it with pleasing imaginations; and seldom appeared to be melancholy, but when some sudden misfortune had just fallen upon him, and even then, in a few moments, he would disentangle himself from his perplexity, adopt the subject of conversation, and apply his mind wholly to the objects that others presented to it.

This life, unhappy as it may be already imagined, was yet imbittered in 1738 with new calamities. The death of the Queen deprived him of all the prospects of preferment, with which he so long entertained his imagination; and, as Sir Robert Walpole had before given him reason to believe that he never intended the performance of his promise, he was now abandoned again to fortune.

He was, however, at that time, supported by a friend; and as it was not his custom to look out for distant calamities, or to feel any other pain than that which forced itself upon his senses, he was not much afflicted at his loss, and perhaps comforted himself that his pension would be now continued without the annual tribute of a panegyrick.

Another expectation contributed likewise to support him: he had taken a resolution to write a second tragedy upon the story of Sir Thomas Overbury, in which he preserved a few lines of his former play, but made a total alteration of the plan, added new incidents, and introduced new characters; so that it was a new tragedy, not a revival of the former.

Many of his friends blamed him for not making choice of another subject; but, in vindication of himself, he asserted that it was not easy to find a better; and that he thought it his interest to extinguish the memory of the first tragedy, which he could only do by writing one less defective upon the same story; by which he should entirely defeat the artifice of the booksellers, who, after the death of any author of reputation, are always industrious to swell his works, by uniting his worst productions with his best.

In the execution of this scheme however he proceeded but slowly, and probably only employed himself upon it when he could find no other amusement; but he pleased himself with counting the profits, and perhaps imagined that the theatrical reputation which he was about to acquire would be equivalent to all that he had lost by the death of his patroness.

He did not, in confidence of his approaching riches, neglect the measures proper to secure the continuance of his pension, though some of his favourers thought him culpable for omitting to write on her death; but, on her birthday next year he gave a proof of the solidity of his judgment, and the power of his genius. He knew that the track of elegy had been so long beaten, that it was impossible to travel in it without treading in the footsteps of those who had gone before him; and that there-fore it was necessary that he might distinguish himself from the herd of encomiasts, to find out some new walk of funeral panegyrick.

This difficult task he performed in such a manner that his poem may be justly ranked among the best pieces that the death of princes has produced. By transferring the mention of her death to her birthday, he has formed a happy combination of topicks, which any other man would have thought it very difficult to connect in one view, but which he has united in such a manner that the relation between them appears natural; and it may be justly said, that what no other man would have thought on, it now appears scarcely possible for any man to miss.

The beauty of this peculiar combination of images is so masterly that it is sufficient to set this poem above censure; and therefore it is not necessary to mention many other delicate touches which may be found in it, and which would deservedly be admired in any other performance.

To these proofs of his genius may be added, from the same poem, an instance of his prudence, an excellence for which he was not so often distinguished; he does not forget to remind the King, in the most delicate and artful manner, of continuing his pension.

With regard to the success of this address, he was, for some time in suspense, but was in no great degree solicitous about it; and continued his labour upon his new tragedy with great tranquillity, till the friend, who had for a considerable time supported him, removing his family to another place, took occasion to dismiss him. It then became necessary to inquire more diligently what was determined in his affair, having reason to suspect that no great favour was intended him, because he had not received his pension at the usual time.

It is said that he did not take those methods of retrieving his interest which were most likely to succeed; and some of those who were employed in the exchequer cautioned him against too much violence in his proceedings: but Mr Savage, who seldom regulated his conduct by the advice of others, gave way to his passion, and demanded of Sir Robert Walpole, at his levee, the reason of the distinction that was made between him and the other pensioners of the queen, with a degree of roughness, which perhaps determined him to withdraw what had been only delayed.

Whatever was the crime of which he was accused or suspected, and whatever influence was employed against him, he received, soon after, an account that took from him all hopes of regaining his pension; and he had now no prospect of subsistence but from his play, and he knew no way of living for the time required to finish it.

So peculiar were the misfortunes of this man, deprived of an estate and title by a particular law, exposed and abandoned by a mother, defrauded by a mother of a fortune which his father had allotted him, he entered the world without a friend; and though his abilities forced themselves into esteem and reputation, he was never able to obtain any real advantage, and whatever prospects arose, were always intercepted as he began to approach them. The King's intentions in his favour were frustrated; his dedication to the prince, whose generosity on every other occasion was eminent, procured him no reward; Sir Robert Walpole, who valued himself upon keeping his promise to others, broke it to him without regret; and the bounty of the Queen was, after her death, withdrawn from him, and from him only.

Such were his misfortunes, which yet he bore, not only with decency but with cheerfulness; nor was his gaiety clouded even by his last disappointments, though he was, in a short time, reduced to the lowest degree of distress, and often wanted both lodging and food. At this time he gave another instance of the insurmountable obstinacy of his spirit: his clothes were worn out; and he received notice that at a coffee-house some clothes and linen were left for him: the person who sent them did not, I believe, inform him to whom he was to be obliged that he might spare the perplexity of acknowledging the benefit; but though the offer was so far generous, it was made with some neglect of ceremonies, which Mr Savage so much resented that he refused the present, and declined to enter the house till the clothes that had been designed for him were taken away.

His distress was now publickly known, and his friends therefore thought it proper to concert some measures for his relief; and one of them wrote a letter to him, in which he expressed his concern 'for the miserable withdrawing of his pension;' and gave him hopes that, in a short time, he should find himself supplied with a competence, 'without any dependence on those little creatures which we are pleased to call the great.'

The scheme proposed for this happy and independent subsistence was that he should retire into Wales, and receive an allowance of fifty pounds a year, to be raised by a subscription, on which he was to live privately in a cheap place, without aspiring any more to affluence, or having any further care of reputation.

This offer Mr Savage gladly accepted, though with intentions very different from those of his friends; for they proposed that he should continue an exile from London for ever, and spend all the remaining part of his life at Swansea; but he designed only to take the opportunity, which their scheme offered him, of retreating for a short time that he might prepare his play for the stage, and his other works for the press, and then to return to London to exhibit his tragedy, and live upon the profits of his own labour.

With regard to his works, he proposed very great improvements, which would have required much time, or great application; and, when he had finished them, he designed to do justice to his subscribers, by publishing them according to his proposals.

As he was ready to entertain himself with future pleasures, he had planned out a scheme of life for the country, of which he had no knowledge but from pastorals and songs. He imagined that he should be transported to scenes of flowery felicity, like those which one poet has reflected to another; and had projected a perpetual round of innocent pleasures, of which he suspected no interruption from pride, or ignorance, or brutality.

With these expectations he was so enchanted that when he was once gently reproached by a friend for submitting to live upon a subscription, and advised rather by a resolute exertion of his abilities to support himself, he could not bear to debar himself from the happiness which was to be found in the calm of a cottage, or lose the opportunity of listening, without intermission, to the melody of the nightingale, which he believed was to be heard from every bramble, and which he did not fail to mention as a very important part of the happiness of a country life.

While this scheme was ripening, his friends directed him to take a lodging in the liberties of the Fleet, that he might be secure from his creditors, and sent him, every Monday, a guinea, which he commonly spent before the next morning, and trusted, after his usual manner, the remaining part of the week to the bounty of fortune.

He now began very sensibly to feel the miseries of dependence. Those by whom he was to be supported began to prescribe to him with an air of authority, which he knew not how decently to resent, nor patiently to bear; and he soon discovered, from the conduct of most of his subscribers, that he was yet in the hands of 'little creatures.'

Of the insolence that he was obliged to suffer, he gave many instances, of which none appeared to raise his indignation to a greater height than the method which was taken of furnishing him with clothes. Instead of consulting him, and allowing him to send a tailor his orders for what they thought proper to allow him, they proposed to send for a tailor to take his measure, and then to consult how they should equip him.

This treatment was not very delicate, nor was it such as Savage's humanity would have suggested to him on a like occasion; but it had scarcely deserved mention, had it not, by affecting him in an uncommon degree, shown the peculiarity of his character. Upon hearing the design that was formed, he came to the lodging of a friend with the most violent agonies of rage; and, being asked what it could be that gave him such disturbance, he replied, with the utmost vehemence of indignation, 'that they had sent for a tailor to measure him.'

How the affair ended was never inquired, for fear of renewing his uneasiness. It is probable that, upon recollection, he submitted with a good grace to what he could not avoid, and that he discovered no resentment where he had no power.

He was however not humbled to implicit and universal compliance; for when the gentleman, who had first informed him of the design to support him by a subscription, attempted to procure a reconciliation with the Lord Tyrconnel, he could by no means be prevailed upon to comply with the measures that were proposed.

A letter was written for him* to Sir William Lemon, to prevail upon him to interpose his good offices with Lord Tyrconnel, in which he solicited Sir William's assistance 'for a man who really needed it as much as any man could well do;' and informed him, that he was retiring 'for ever to a place where he should no more trouble his relations, friends, or enemies;' he confessed, that his passion had betrayed him to some conduct, with regard to Lord Tyrconnel, for which he could not but heartily ask his

* By Mr Pope.

pardon; and as he imagined Lord Tyrconnel's passion might be yet so high that he would not 'receive a letter from him,' begged that Sir William would endeavour to soften him; and expressed his hopes that he would comply with his request, and that 'so small a relation would not harden his heart against him.'

That any man should presume to dictate a letter to him, was not very agreeable to Mr Savage; and, therefore, he was, before he had opened it, not much inclined to approve it. But when he read it, he found it contained sentiments entirely opposite to his own, and, as he asserted, to the truth, and, therefore, instead of copying it, wrote his friend a letter full of masculine resentment and warm expostulations. He very justly observed, that the style was too supplicatory, and the representation too abject, and that he ought, at least, to have made him complain with 'the dignity of a gentleman in distress.' He declared that he would not write the paragraph in which he was to ask Lord Tyrconnel's pardon; for 'he despised his pardon, and therefore could not heartily, and would not hypocritically, ask it.' He remarked, that his friend made a very unreasonable distinction between himself and him; for, says he, when you mention men of high rank 'in your own character,' they are, 'those little creatures whom we are pleased to call the great;' but when you address them 'in mine,' no servility is sufficiently humble. He then, with great propriety, explained the ill consequences which might be expected from such a letter, which his relations would print in their own defence, and which would for ever be produced as a full answer to all that he should allege against them; for he always intended to publish a minute account of the treatment which he had received. It is to be remembered, to the honour of the gentleman by whom this letter was drawn up, that he yielded to Mr Savage's reasons, and agreed that it ought to be suppressed.

After many alterations and delays, a subscription was at length raised, which did not amount to fifty pounds a year, though twenty were paid by one gentleman; such was the generosity of mankind, that what had been done by a player without solicitation, could not now be effected by application and interest; and Savage had a great number to court and to obey for a pension less than that which Mrs Oldfield paid him without exacting any servilities.

Mr Savage however was satisfied, and willing to retire, and was convinced that the allowance, though scanty, would be more than sufficient for him, being now determined to commence a rigid economist, and to live according to the exactest rules of frugality; for nothing was, in his opinion, more contemptible, than a man, who, when he knew his income, exceeded it; and yet he confessed that instances of such folly were too common, and lamented that some men were not to be trusted with their own money.

Full of these salutary resolutions, he left London in July, 1739, having taken leave, with great tenderness, of his friends, and parted from the author of this narrative with tears in his eyes. He was furnished with fifteen guineas, and informed that they would be sufficient, not only for the expense of his journey, but for his support in Wales for some time; and that there remained but little more of the first collection. He promised a strict adherence to his maxims of parsimony, and went away in the stage-coach; nor did his friends expect to hear from him till he informed them of his arrival at Swansea.

But, when they least expected, arrived a letter dated the fourteenth day after his departure, in which he sent them word that he was yet upon the road and without money; and that he therefore could not proceed without a remittance. They then sent him the money that was in their hands, with which he was enabled to reach Bristol, from whence he was to go to Swansea by water.

At Bristol he found an embargo laid upon the shipping, so that he could not immediately obtain a passage; and being, therefore, obliged to stay there some time, he, with his usual felicity, ingratiated himself with many of the principal inhabitants, was invited to their houses, distinguished at their publick feasts, and treated with a regard that gratified his vanity, and therefore easily engaged his affection.

He began, very early after his retirement, to complain of the conduct of his friends in London, and irritated many of them so much by his letters, that they withdrew, however honourably, their contributions; and it is believed, that little more was paid him than the twenty pounds a year, which were allowed him by the gentleman who proposed the subscription.

After some stay at Bristol he retired to Swansea, the place originally proposed for his residence, where he lived about a year, very much dissatisfied with the diminution of his salary; but contracted, as in other places, acquaintance with those who were most distinguished in that country, among whom he has celebrated Mr Powell and Mrs Jones, by some verses which he inserted in the *Gentleman's Magazine*.

Here he completed his tragedy, of which two acts were wanting when he left London; and was desirous of coming to town, to bring it upon the stage. This design was very warmly opposed; and he was advised, by his chief benefactor, to put it into the hands of Mr Thomson and Mr Mallet, that it might be fitted for the stage, and to allow his friends to receive the profits, out of which an annual pension should be paid him.

This proposal he rejected with the utmost contempt. He was

by no means convinced that the judgment of those to whom he was required to submit was superiour to his own. He was now determined, as he expressed it, to be 'no longer kept in leading-strings,' and had no elevated idea of 'his bounty, who proposed to pension him out of the profits of his own labours.'

He attempted in Wales to promote a subscription for his works, and had once hopes of success; but, in a short time afterwards, formed a resolution of leaving that part of the country, to which he thought it not reasonable to be confined, for the gratification of those who, having promised him a liberal income, had no sooner banished him to a remote corner, than they reduced his allowance to a salary scarcely equal to the necessities of life.

His resentment of this treatment, which, in his own opinion at least, he had not deserved, was such that he broke off all correspondence with most of his contributors, and appeared to consider them as persecutors and oppressors; and, in the latter part of his life, declared that their conduct toward him since his departure from London 'had been perfidiousness improving on perfidiousness, and inhumanity on inhumanity.'

It is not to be supposed that the necessities of Mr Savage did not sometimes incite him to satirical exaggerations of the behaviour of those by whom he thought himself reduced to them. But it must be granted that the diminution of his allowance was a great hardship, and that those who withdrew their subscriptions from a man, who, upon the faith of their promise, had gone into a kind of banishment, and abandoned all those by whom he had been before relieved in his distresses, will find it no easy task to vindicate their conduct.

It may be alleged, and perhaps justly, that he was petulant and contemptuous; that he more frequently reproached his subscribers for not giving him more than thanked them for what he received; but it is to be remembered that his conduct, and this is the worst charge that can be drawn up against him, did them no real injury, and that it therefore ought rather to have been pitied than resented; at least, the resentment it might provoke ought to have been generous and manly; epithets which his conduct will hardly deserve, that starves the man whom he has persuaded to put himself into his power.

It might have been reasonably demanded by Savage that they should, before they had taken away what they promised, have replaced him in his former state; that they should have taken no advantages from the situation to which the appearance of their kindness had reduced him, and that he should have been recalled to London before he was abandoned. He might justly represent that he ought to have been considered as a lion in the toils, and demand to be released before the dogs should be loosed upon him.

He endeavoured indeed to release himself, and, with an intent to return to London, went to Bristol, where a repetition of the kindness which he had formerly found invited him to stay. He was not only caressed and treated, but had a collection made for him of about thirty pounds, with which it had been happy if he had immediately departed for London; but his negligence did not suffer him to consider that such proofs of kindness were not often to be expected, and that this ardour of benevolence was, in a great degree, the effect of novelty, and might, probably, be every day less; and therefore he took no care to improve the happy time, but was encouraged by one favour to hope for another, till, at length, generosity was exhausted, and officiousness wearied.

Another part of his misconduct was the practice of prolonging his visits to unseasonable hours, and disconcerting all the families into which he was admitted. This was an errour in a place of commerce, which all the charms of his conversation could not compensate; for what trader would purchase such airy satisfaction by the loss of solid gain, which must be the consequence of midnight merriment, as those hours which were gained at night were generally lost in the morning?

Thus Mr Savage, after the curiosity of the inhabitants was gratified, found the number of his friends daily decreasing perhaps without suspecting for what reason their conduct was altered; for he still continued to harass, with his nocturnal intrusions, those that yet countenanced him, and admitted him to their houses.

But he did not spend all the time of his residence at Bristol, in visits or at taverns; for he sometimes returned to his studies, and began several considerable designs. When he felt an inclination to write, he always retired from the knowledge of his friends, and lay hid in an obscure part of the suburbs, till he found himself again desirous of company, to which it is likely that intervals of absence made him more welcome.

He was always full of his design of returning to London, to bring his tragedy upon the stage; but, having neglected to depart with the money that was raised for him, he could not afterwards procure a sum sufficient to defray the expenses of his journey; nor perhaps would a fresh supply have had any other effect than by putting immediate pleasures in his power, to have driven the thoughts of his journey out of his mind.

While he was thus spending the day in contriving a scheme for the morrow, distress stole upon him by imperceptible degrees. His conduct had already wearied some of those who were at first enamoured of his conversation; but he might perhaps still have devolved to others, whom he might have entertained with equal success, had not the decay of his clothes made it no longer consistent with their vanity to admit him to their tables, or to associate with him in publick places. He now began to find every man from home at whose house he called; and was therefore no longer able to procure the necessaries of life, but wandered about the town, slighted and neglected, in quest of a dinner, which he did not always obtain.

To complete his misery, he was pursued by the officers for small debts which he had contracted; and was therefore obliged to withdraw from the small number of friends from whom he had still reason to hope for favours. His custom was to lie in bed the greatest part of the day, and to go out in the dark with the utmost privacy, and after having paid his visit, return again before morning to his lodging, which was in the garret of an obscure inn.

Being thus excluded on one hand, and confined on the other, he suffered the utmost extremities of poverty, and often fasted so long that he was seized with faintness, and had lost his appetite, not being able to bear the smell of meat, till the action of his stomach was restored by a cordial.

In this distress, he received a remittance of five pounds from London, with which he provided himself a decent coat, and determined to go to London, but unhappily spent his money at a favourite tavern. Thus was he again confined to Bristol, where he was every day hunted by bailiffs. In this exigence he once more found a friend, who sheltered him in his house, though at the usual inconveniencies with which his company was attended; for he could neither be persuaded to go to bed in the night, nor to rise in the day.

It is observable that in these various scenes of misery, he was always disengaged and cheerful: he at some times pursued his studies, and at others continued or enlarged his epistolary correspondence; nor was he ever so far dejected as to endeavour to procure an increase of his allowance by any other methods than accusations and reproaches.

He had now no longer any hopes of assistance from his friends at Bristol, who, as merchants, and by consequence sufficiently studious of profit, cannot be supposed to have looked with much compassion upon negligence and extravagance, or to think any excellence equivalent to a fault of such consequence as neglect of economy. It is natural to imagine that many of those, who would have relieved his real wants, were discouraged from the exertion of their benevolence, by observation of the use which was made of their favours, and conviction that relief would only be momentary, and that the same necessity would quickly return.

At last he quitted the house of his friend, and returned to his lodging at the inn, still intending to set out in a few days for London; but on the 10th of January, 1742–3, having been at supper with two of his friends, he was, at his return to his lodgings, arrested for a debt of about eight pounds which he owed at a coffee-house, and conducted to the house of a sheriff's officer. The account which he gives of this misfortune, in a letter to one of the gentlemen with whom he had supped, is too remarkable to be omitted.

'It was not a little unfortunate for me that I spent yesterday's evening with you; because the hour hindered me from entering on my new lodging; however, I have now got one, but such an one as I believe nobody would choose.

'I was arrested at the suit of Mrs Read, just as I was going up stairs to bed, at Mr Bowyer's; but taken in so private a manner that I believe nobody at the White Lion is apprised of it; though

I let the officers know the strength, or rather weakness, of my pocket, yet they treated me with the utmost civility; and even when they conducted me to confinement, it was in such a manner that I verily believe I could have escaped, which I would rather be ruined than have done, notwithstanding the whole amount of my finances was but threepence halfpenny.

'In the first place, I must insist, that you will industriously conceal this from Mrs S——s, because I would not have her good-nature suffer that pain which, I know, she would be apt to feel on this occasion.

'Next, I conjure you, dear Sir, by all the ties of friendship, by no means to have one uneasy thought on my account; but to have the same pleasantry of countenance, and unruffled serenity of mind, which (God be praised!) I have in this, and have had in a much severer calamity. Furthermore, I charge you, if you value my friendship as truly as I do yours, not to utter, or even harbour, the least resentment against Mrs Read. I believe she has ruined me, but I freely forgive her; and (though I will never more have any intimacy with her) I would, at a due distance, rather do her an act of good, than ill will. Lastly, (pardon the expression,) I absolutely command you not to offer me any pecuniary assistance, nor to attempt getting me any from any one of your friends. At another time, or on any other occasion, you may, dear friend, be well assured, I would rather write to you in the submissive style of a request, than that of a peremptory command.

'However, that my truly valuable friend may not think I am too proud to ask a favour, let me intreat you to let me have your boy to attend me for this day, not only for the sake of saving me the expense of porters, but for the delivery of some letters to people whose names I would not have known to strangers.

'The civil treatment I have thus far met from those whose prisoner I am makes me thankful to the Almighty, that, though he has thought fit to visit me (on my birth-night) with affliction, yet (such is his great goodness!) my affliction is not without alleviating circumstances. I murmur not; but am all resignation to the divine will. As to the world, I hope that I shall be endued by heaven with that presence of mind, that serene dignity in misfortune, that constitutes the character of a true nobleman; a dignity far beyond that of coronets; a nobility arising from the just principles of philosophy, refined and exalted by those of Christianity.'

He continued five days at the officer's, in hopes that he should be able to procure bail and avoid the necessity of going to prison. The state in which he passed his time, and the treatment which he received, are very justly expressed by him in a letter which he wrote to a friend: 'The whole day,' says he, 'has been employed in various people's filling my head with their foolish chimerical systems, which has obliged me coolly (as far as nature will admit) to digest, and accommodate myself to, every different person's way of thinking; hurried from one wild system to another, till it has quite made a chaos of my imagination, and nothing done – promised – disappointed – ordered to send, every hour, from one part of the town to the other.'

When his friends, who had hitherto caressed and applauded, found that to give bail and pay the debt was the same, they all refused to preserve him from a prison at the expense of eight pounds; and therefore after having been for some time at the officer's house, 'at an immense expense,' as he observes in his letter, he was at length removed to Newgate.

This expense he was enabled to support by the generosity of Mr Nash, at Bath, who, upon receiving from him an account of his condition, immediately sent him five guineas, and promised to promote his subscription at Bath with all his interest.

By his removal to Newgate, he obtained at least a freedom from suspense, and rest from the disturbing vicissitudes of hope and disappointment; he now found that his friends were only companions, who were willing to share his gaiety, but not to partake of his misfortunes; and therefore he no longer expected any assistance from them.

It must however be observed of one gentleman that he offered to release him by paying the debt; but that Mr Savage would not consent, I suppose, because he thought he had before been too burdensome to him.

He was offered by some of his friends that a collection should be made for his enlargement; but he 'treated the proposal,' and declared 'he should again treat it, with disdain. As to writing any mendicant letters, he had too high a spirit, and determined only to write to some ministers of state, to try to regain his pension.'

He continued to complain* of those that had sent him into the country, and objected to them that he had 'lost the profits of his play, which had been finished three years:' and in another letter declares his resolution to publish a pamphlet, that the world might know how 'he had been used.'

This pamphlet was never written; for he, in a very short time, recovered his usual tranquillity, and cheerfully applied himself to more inoffensive studies. He indeed steadily declared that he was promised a yearly allowance of fifty pounds, and never received half the sum; but he seemed to resign himself to that

---

* In a letter after his confinement.

as well as to other misfortunes, and lose the remembrance of it in his amusements and employments.

The cheerfulness with which he bore his confinement appears from the following letter, which he wrote, January the 30th, to one of his friends in London.

'I now write to you from my confinement in Newgate, where I have been ever since Monday last was se'nnight, and where I enjoy myself with much more tranquillity than I have known for upwards of a twelvemonth past; having a room entirely to myself, and pursuing the amusement of my poetical studies, uninterrupted, and agreeable to my mind. I thank the Almighty, I am now all collected in myself; and, though my person is in confinement, my mind can expatiate on ample and useful subjects with all the freedom imaginable. I am now more conversant with the Nine than ever, and if, instead of a Newgate-bird, I may be allowed to be a bird of the Muses, I assure you, sir, I sing very freely in my cage; sometimes, indeed, in the plaintive notes of the nightingale; but at others in the cheerful strains of the lark.'

In another letter he observes that he ranges from one subject to another, without confining himself to any particular task; and that he was employed one week upon one attempt, and the next upon another.

Surely the fortitude of this man deserves at least to be mentioned with applause; and, whatever faults may be imputed to him, the virtue of suffering well cannot be denied him. The two powers which, in the opinion of Epictetus, constituted a wise man, are those of bearing and forbearing; which cannot indeed be affirmed to have been equally possessed by Savage; and indeed the want of one obliged him very frequently to practise the other.

He was treated by Mr Dagge, the keeper of the prison, with great humanity; was supported by him at his own table, without any certainty of recompense; had a room to himself, to which he could at any time retire from all disturbance; was allowed to stand at the door of the prison, and sometimes taken out into the fields; so that he suffered fewer hardships in prison than he had been accustomed to undergo in the greatest part of his life.

The keeper did not confine his benevolence to a gentle execution of his office, but made some overtures to the creditor for his release, though without effect; and continued, during the whole time of his imprisonment, to treat him with the utmost tenderness and civility.

Virtue is undoubtedly most laudable in that state which makes it most difficult; and, therefore, the humanity of a gaoler certainly deserves this publick attestation; and the man whose heart has not been hardened by such an employment may be justly proposed as a pattern of benevolence. If an inscription was once engraved, 'to the honest toll-gatherer,' less honours ought not to be paid 'to the tender gaoler.'

Mr Savage very frequently received visits, and sometimes presents, from his acquaintances; but they did not amount to a subsistence, for the greater part of which he was indebted to the generosity of this keeper; but these favours, however they might endear to him the particular persons from whom he received them, were very far from impressing upon his mind any advantageous ideas of the people of Bristol, and therefore he thought he could not more properly employ himself in prison, than in writing a poem, called *London and Bristol Delineated*.*

* The author preferred this title to that of London and Bristol compared; which, when he began the piece, he intended to prefix to it.

When he had brought this poem to its present state, which, without considering the chasm, is not perfect, he wrote to London an account of his design, and informed his friend, that he was determined to print it with his name; but enjoined him not to communicate his intention to his Bristol acquaintance. The gentleman, surprised at his resolution, endeavoured to dissuade him from publishing it, at least from prefixing his name; and declared that he could not reconcile the injunction of secrecy with his resolution to own it at its first appearance. To this Mr Savage returned an answer agreeable to his character, in the following terms:

'I received yours this morning; and not without a little surprise at the contents. To answer a question with a question, you ask me concerning *London and Bristol*, Why will I add *Delineated*? Why did Mr Wollaston add the same word to his *Religion of Nature?* I suppose that it was his will and pleasure to add it in his case; and it is mine to do so in my own. You are pleased to tell me that you understand not why secrecy is enjoined, and yet I intend to set my name to it. My answer is – I have my private reasons, which I am not obliged to explain to any one. You doubt my friend Mr S—— would not approve of it – And what is it to me whether he does or not? Do you imagine that Mr S——is to dictate to me? If any man who calls himself my friend should assume such an air, I would spurn at his friendship with contempt. You say, I seem to think so by not letting him know it. – And suppose I do, what then? Perhaps I can give reasons for that disapprobation, very foreign from what you would imagine. You go on in saying, suppose I should not put my name to it – My answer is, that I will not suppose any such thing, being determined to the contrary: neither, sir, would I have you suppose, that I applied to you for want of another

press: nor would I have you imagine, that I owe Mr S——
obligations which I do not.'

Such was his imprudence, and such his obstinate adherence
to his own resolutions, however absurd! A prisoner! supported
by charity! and, whatever insults he might have received during
the latter part of his stay in Bristol, once caressed, esteemed,
and presented with a liberal collection, he could forget, on a
sudden, his danger and his obligations, to gratify the petulance
of his wit, or the eagerness of his resentment, and publish a
satire, by which he might reasonably expect that he should alien-
ate those who then supported him, and provoke those whom
he could neither resist nor escape.

This resolution, from the execution of which it is probable
that only his death could have hindered him, is sufficient to
show how much he disregarded all considerations that opposed
his present passions, and how readily he hazarded all future
advantages for any immediate gratifications. Whatever was his
predominant inclination, neither hope nor fear hindered him
from complying with it; nor had opposition any other effect
than to heighten his ardour, and irritate his vehemence.

This performance was, however, laid aside, while he was
employed in soliciting assistance from several great persons; and
one interruption succeeding another hindered him from supplying the chasm, and perhaps from retouching the other parts,
which he can hardly be imagined to have finished in his own
opinion: for it is very unequal, and some of the lines are rather
inserted to rhyme to others, than to support or improve the
sense; but the first and last parts are worked up with great spirit
and elegance.

His time was spent in the prison, for the most part, in study,
or in receiving visits; but sometimes he descended to lower

amusements, and diverted himself in the kitchen with the conversation of the criminals: for it was not pleasing to him to be much without company; and, though he was very capable of a judicious choice, he was often contented with the first that offered: for this he was sometimes reproved by his friends, who found him surrounded with felons; but the reproof was on that, as on other occasions, thrown away; he continued to gratify himself, and to set very little value on the opinion of others.

But here, as in every other scene of his life, he made use of such opportunities as occurred of benefiting those who were more miserable than himself, and was always ready to perform any office of humanity to his fellow-prisoners.

He had now ceased from corresponding with any of his subscribers except one, who yet continued to remit him the twenty pounds a year which he had promised him, and by whom it was expected that he would have been in a very short time enlarged, because he had directed the keeper to inquire after the state of his debts.

However, he took care to enter his name according to the forms of the court, that the creditor might be obliged to make him some allowance, if he was continued a prisoner, and, when on that occasion he appeared in the hall, was treated with very unusual respect.

But the resentment of the city was afterwards raised by some accounts that had been spread of the satire; and he was informed that some of the merchants intended to pay the allowance which the law required, and to detain him a prisoner at their own expense. This he treated as an empty menace; and, perhaps, might have hastened the publication, only to show how much he was superiour to their insults, had not all his schemes been suddenly destroyed.

When he had been six months in prison, he received from one of his friends, in whose kindness he had the greatest confidence, and on whose assistance he chiefly depended, a letter, that contained a charge of very atrocious ingratitude, drawn up in such terms as sudden resentment dictated. Henley, in one of his advertisements, had mentioned 'Pope's treatment of Savage.' This was supposed by Pope to be the consequence of a complaint made by Savage to Henley, and was, therefore, mentioned by him with much resentment. Mr Savage returned a very solemn protestation of his innocence, but however appeared much disturbed at the accusation. Some days afterwards he was seized with a pain in his back and side, which, as it was not violent, was not suspected to be dangerous; but, growing daily more languid and dejected, on the 25th of July he confined himself to his room, and a fever seized his spirits. The symptoms grew every day more formidable, but his condition did not enable him to procure any assistance. The last time that the keeper saw him was on July the 31st, 1743; when Savage, seeing him at his bedside, said with an uncommon earnestness, 'I have something to say to you, sir;' but, after a pause, moved his hand in a melancholy manner; and, finding himself unable to recollect what he was going to communicate, said, ''Tis gone!' The keeper soon after left him; and the next morning he died. He was buried in the church-yard of St Peter, at the expense of the keeper.

Such were the life and death of Richard Savage, a man equally distinguished by his virtues and vices; and at once remarkable for his weaknesses and abilities.

He was of a middle stature, of a thin habit of body, a long visage, coarse features, and melancholy aspect; of a grave and manly deportment, a solemn dignity of mien, but which, upon a nearer acquaintance, softened into an engaging easiness of manners. His walk was slow, and his voice tremulous and mournful. He was easily excited to smiles, but very seldom provoked to laughter.

His mind was in an uncommon degree vigorous and active. His judgment was accurate, his apprehension quick, and his memory so tenacious, that he was frequently observed to know what he had learned from others, in a short time, better than those by whom he was informed; and could frequently recollect incidents, with all their combination of circumstances, which few would have regarded at the present time, but which the quickness of his apprehension impressed upon him. He had the peculiar felicity that his attention never deserted him; he was present to every object, and regardful of the most trifling occurrences. He had the art of escaping from his own reflections, and accommodating himself to every new scene.

To this quality is to be imputed the extent of his knowledge, compared with the small time which he spent in visible endeavours to acquire it. He mingled in cursory conversation with the same steadiness of attention as others apply to a lecture; and, amidst the appearance of thoughtless gaiety, lost no new idea that was started, nor any hint that could be improved. He had therefore made in coffee-houses the same proficiency as others in their closets: and it is remarkable that the writings of a man of little education and little reading have an air of learning scarcely to be found in any other performances, but which, perhaps, as often obscures as embellishes them.

His judgment was eminently exact, both with regard to writings and to men. The knowledge of life was indeed his chief attainment; and it is not without some satisfaction that I can produce the suffrage of Savage in favour of human nature, of which he never appeared to entertain such odious ideas as some, who perhaps had neither his judgment nor experience, have published, either in ostentation of their sagacity, vindication of their crimes, or gratification of their malice.

His method of life particularly qualified him for conversation, of which he knew how to practise all the graces. He was never vehement or loud, but at once modest and easy, open and respectful; his language was vivacious and elegant, and equally happy upon grave or humorous subjects. He was generally censured for not knowing when to retire; but that was not the defect of his judgment, but of his fortune: when he left his company, he was frequently to spend the remaining part of the night in the street, or at least was abandoned to gloomy reflections, which it is not strange that he delayed as long as he could; and sometimes forgot that he gave others pain to avoid it himself.

It cannot be said that he made use of his abilities for the direction of his own conduct: an irregular and dissipated manner of life had made him the slave of every passion that happened to be excited by the presence of its object, and that slavery to his passions reciprocally produced a life irregular and dissipated. He was not master of his own motions, nor could promise any thing for the next day.

With regard to his economy, nothing can be added to the relation of his life. He appeared to think himself born to be supported by others, and dispensed from all necessity of providing for himself; he therefore never prosecuted any scheme of advantage, nor endeavoured even to secure the profits which his writings might have afforded him. His temper was, in consequence of the dominion of his passions, uncertain and capricious; he was easily engaged, and easily disgusted; but he is accused of retaining his hatred more tenaciously than his benevolence.

He was compassionate both by nature and principle, and always ready to perform offices of humanity; but when he was provoked (and very small offences were sufficient to provoke him) he would prosecute his revenge with the utmost acrimony till his passion had subsided.

His friendship was therefore of little value; for, though he was zealous in the support or vindication of those whom he loved, yet it was always dangerous to trust him, because he considered himself as discharged, by the first quarrel, from all ties of honour or gratitude; and would betray those secrets which, in the warmth of confidence, had been imparted to him. This practice drew upon him an universal accusation of ingratitude: nor can it be denied that he was very ready to set himself free from the load of an obligation; for he could not bear to conceive himself in a state of dependence, his pride being equally powerful with his other passions, and appearing in the form of insolence at one time, and of vanity at another. Vanity, the most innocent species of pride, was most frequently predominant: he could not easily leave off, when he had once begun to mention himself or his works; nor ever read his verses without stealing his eyes from the page, to discover, in the faces of his audience, how they were affected with any favourite passage.

A kinder name than that of vanity ought to be given to the delicacy with which he was always careful to separate his own merit from every other man's, and to reject that praise to which he had no claim. He did not forget, in mentioning his perform-ances, to mark every line that had been suggested or amended; and was so accurate, as to relate that he owed three words in the *Wanderer* to the advice of his friends.

His veracity was questioned, but with little reason; his accounts, though not indeed always the same, were generally consistent. When he loved any man, he suppressed all his faults; and, when he had been offended by him, concealed all his virtues; but his characters were generally true, so far as he proceeded; though it cannot be denied, that his partiality might have sometimes the effect of falsehood.

In cases indifferent, he was zealous for virtue, truth, and justice; he knew very well the necessity of goodness to the present and future happiness of mankind; nor is there perhaps any writer who has less endeavoured to please by flattering the appetites, or perverting the judgment.

As an author therefore and he now ceases to influence mankind in any other character, if one piece which he had resolved to suppress be excepted, he has very little to fear from the strictest moral or religious censure. And though he may not be altogether secure against the objections of the critick, it must however be acknowledged, that his works are the productions of a genius truly poetical; and, what many writers who have been more lavishly applauded cannot boast, that they have an original air, which has no resemblance of any foregoing writer, that the versification and sentiments have a cast peculiar to themselves, which no man can imitate with success, because what was nature in Savage would in another be affectation. It must be confessed that his descriptions are striking, his images animated, his fictions justly imagined, and his allegories artfully pursued; that his diction is elevated, though sometimes forced, and his numbers sonorous and majestick, though frequently sluggish and encumbered. Of his style, the general fault is harshness, and its general excellence is dignity: of his sentiments, the prevailing beauty is simplicity, and uniformity the prevailing defect.

For his life or for his writings, none who candidly consider his fortune will think an apology either necessary or difficult.

If he was not always sufficiently instructed in his subject, his knowledge was, at least, greater than could have been attained by others in the same state. If his works were sometimes unfinished, accuracy cannot reasonably be expected from a man oppressed with want, which he has no hope of relieving but by a speedy publication. The insolence and resentment of which he is accused were not easily to be avoided by a great mind, irritated by perpetual hardships, and constrained hourly to return the spurns of contempt, and repress the insolence of prosperity; and vanity may surely be readily pardoned in him, to whom life afforded no other comforts than barren praises, and the consciousness of deserving them.

Those are no proper judges of his conduct, who have slumbered away their time on the down of plenty; nor will any wise man presume to say, 'Had I been in Savage's condition, I should have lived or written better than Savage.'

This relation will not be wholly without its use, if those, who languish under any part of his sufferings, shall be enabled to fortify their patience, by reflecting that they feel only those afflictions from which the abilities of Savage did not exempt him; or if those, who, in confidence of superiour capacities or attainments, disregard the common maxims of life, shall be reminded, that nothing will supply the want of prudence, and that negligence and irregularity, long continued, will make knowledge useless, wit ridiculous, and genius contemptible.

BIOGRAPHY

−Quid sit pulchrum, quid turpe, quid utile, quid non,
Plenius ac melius Chrysippo et Crantore dicit.

Hor. Lib. i. Epist. ii. 3.

Whose works the beautiful and base contain,
Of vice and virtue more instructive rules,
Than all the sober sages of the schools.

Francis

ALL joy or sorrow for the happiness or calamities of others is produced by an act of the imagination, that realizes the event, however fictitious, or approximates it, however remote, by placing us, for a time, in the condition of him whose fortune we contemplate; so that we feel, while the deception lasts, whatever motions would be excited by the same good or evil happening to ourselves.

Our passions are therefore more strongly moved, in proportion as we can more readily adopt the pains or pleasure proposed to our minds, by recognising them as once our own, or considering them as naturally incident to our state of life. It is not easy for the most artful writer to give us an interest in happiness or misery, which we think ourselves never likely to feel, and with which we have never yet been made acquainted. Histories of the downfall of kingdoms, and revolutions of empires, are read with great tranquillity; the imperial tragedy pleases common auditors only by its pomp of ornament, and grandeur of ideas; and the man whose faculties have been engrossed by business, and whose heart never fluttered but at the rise or fall of the stocks, wonders how the attention can be seized, or the affection agitated, by a tale of love.

Those parallel circumstances and kindred images, to which

we readily conform our minds, are, above all other writings, to be found in narratives of the lives of particular persons; and therefore no species of writing seems more worthy of cultivation than biography, since none can be more delightful or more useful, none can more certainly enchain the heart by irresistible interest, or more widely diffuse instruction to every diversity of condition.

The general and rapid narratives of history, which involve a thousand fortunes in the business of a day, and complicate innumerable incidents in one great transaction, afford few lessons applicable to private life, which derives its comforts and its wretchedness from the right or wrong management of things, which nothing but their frequency makes considerable, *Parva si non fiunt quotidie*, says Pliny, and which can have no place in those relations which never descend below the consultation of senates, the motions of armies, and the schemes of conspirators.

I have often thought that there has rarely passed a life of which a judicious and faithful narrative would not be useful. For, not only every man has, in the mighty mass of the world, great numbers in the same condition with himself, to whom his mistakes and miscarriages, escapes and expedients, would be of immediate and apparent use; but there is such an uniformity in the state of man, considered apart from adventitious and separable decorations and disguises; that there is scarce any possibility of good or ill, but is common to human kind. A great part of the time of those who are placed at the greatest distance by fortune, or by temper, must unavoidably pass in the same manner; and though, when the claims of nature are satisfied, caprice, and vanity, and accident, begin to produce discriminations and peculiarities, yet the eye is not very heedful or quick, which cannot discover the same causes still terminating their influence in the same effects, though sometimes accelerated, sometimes retarded, or perplexed by multiplied combinations. We are all prompted by the same motives, all deceived by the same fallacies, all animated by hope, obstructed by danger, entangled by desire, and seduced by pleasure.

It is frequently objected to relations of particular lives, that they are not distinguished by any striking or wonderful vicissitudes. The scholar who passed his life among his books, the merchant who conducted only his own affairs, the priest, whose sphere of action was not extended beyond that of his duty, are considered as no proper objects of publick regard, however they might have excelled in their several stations, whatever might have been their learning, integrity, and piety. But this notion arises from false measures of excellence and dignity, and must be eradicated by considering, that in the esteem of uncorrupted reason, what is of most use is of most value.

It is indeed not improper to take honest advantages of prejudice, and to gain attention by a celebrated name; but the business of the biographer is often to pass slightly over those performances and incidents, which produce vulgar greatness, to lead the thoughts into domestick privacies, and display the minute details of daily life, where exterior appendages are cast aside, and men excel each other only by prudence and by virtue. The account of Thuanus is, with great propriety, said by its author to have been written, that it might lay open to posterity the private and familiar character of that man, *cujus ingenium et candorem ex ipsius scriptis sunt olim semper miraturi*, whose candour and genius will to the end of time be by his writings preserved in admiration.

There are many invisible circumstances which, whether we read as inquirers after natural or moral knowledge, whether we intend to enlarge our science, or increase our virtue, are more important than publick occurrences. Thus Sallust, the great master of nature, has not forgot, in his account of Catiline, to remark that *his walk was now quick, and again slow*, as an indication of a mind revolving something with violent commotion. Thus the story of Melancthon affords a striking lecture on the value of time, by informing us, that when he made an appointment, he expected not only the hour, but the minute to be fixed, that the day might not run out in the idleness of suspense: and all the plans and enterprises of De Witt are now of less importance to the world, than that part of his personal character, which represents him as *careful of his health, and negligent of his life*.

But biography has often been allotted to writers who seem very little acquainted with the nature of their task, or very negligent about the performance. They rarely afford any other account than might be collected from publick papers, but imagine themselves writing a life when they exhibit a chronological series of actions or preferments; and so little regard the manners or behaviour of their heroes, that more knowledge may be gained of a man's real character, by a short conversation with one of his servants, than from a formal and studied narrative, begun with his pedigree, and ended with his funeral.

If now and then they condescend to inform the world of particular facts, they are not always so happy as to select the most important. I know not well what advantage posterity can receive from the only circumstance by which Tickell has distinguished Addison from the rest of mankind, *the irregularity of his pulse:* nor can I think myself overpaid for the time spent in reading the life of Malherbes, by being enabled to relate, after the learned biographer, that Malherbes had two predominant opinions; one, that the looseness of a single woman might destroy all her boast of ancient descent; the other, that the French beggars made use very improperly and barbarously of the phrase *noble gentleman*, because either word included the sense of both.

There are, indeed, some natural reasons why these narratives are often written by such as were not likely to give much instruction or delight, and why most accounts of particular persons are barren and useless. If a life be delayed till interest and envy are at an end, we may hope for impartiality, but must expect little intelligence; for the incidents which give excellence to biography are of a volatile and evanescent kind, such as soon escape the memory, and are rarely transmitted by tradition. We know how few can portray a living acquaintance, except by his most prominent and observable particularities, and the grosser features of his mind; and it may be easily imagined how much of this little knowledge may be lost in imparting it, and how soon a succession of copies will lose all resemblance of the original.

If the biographer writes from personal knowledge, and makes haste to gratify the publick curiosity, there is danger lest his interest, his fear, his gratitude, or his tenderness, overpower his fidelity, and tempt him to conceal, if not to invent. There are many who think it an act of piety to hide the faults or failings of their friends, even when they can no longer suffer by their detection; we therefore see whole ranks of characters adorned with uniform panegyrick, and not to be known from one another, but by extrinsick and casual circumstances. 'Let me remember,' says Hale, 'when I find myself inclined to pity a criminal, that there is likewise a pity due to the country.' If we owe regard to the memory of the dead, there is yet more respect to be paid to knowledge, to virtue, and to truth.

AUTOBIOGRAPHY

B iography is, of the various kinds of narrative writing, that which is most eagerly read, and most easily applied to the purposes of life.

In romances, when the wide field of possibility lies open to invention, the incidents may easily be made more numerous, the vicissitudes more sudden, and the events more wonderful; but from the time of life when fancy begins to be overruled by reason and corrected by experience, the most artful tale raises little curiosity when it is known to be false,* though it may, perhaps, be sometimes read as a model of a neat or elegant style, not for the sake of knowing what it contains, but how it is written; or those that are weary of themselves, may have recourse to it as a pleasing dream, of which, when they awake, they voluntarily dismiss the images from their minds.

The examples and events of history press, indeed, upon the mind with the weight of truth; but when they are reposited in the memory, they are oftener employed for show than use, and

---

* It is somewhere recorded of a retired citizen, that he was in the habit of again and again perusing the incomparable story of Robinson Crusoe without a suspicion of its authenticity. At length a friend assured him of its being a work of fiction. What you say, replied the old man mournfully, may be true; but your information has taken away the only comfort of my age.

rather diversify conversation than regulate life. Few are engaged in such scenes as give them opportunities of growing wiser by the downfal of statesmen or the defeat of generals. The stratagems of war, and the intrigues of courts, are read by far the greater part of mankind with the same indifference as the adventures of fabled heroes, or the revolutions of a fairy region. Between false-hood and useless truth there is little difference. As gold which he cannot spend will make no man rich, so knowledge which he cannot apply will make no man wise.

The mischievous consequences of vice and folly, of irregular desires and predominant passions, are best discovered by those relations which are levelled with the general surface of life, which tell not how any man became great, but how he was made happy; not how he lost the favour of his prince, but how he became discontented with himself.

Those relations are, therefore, commonly of most value in which the writer tells his own story. He that recounts the life of another, commonly dwells most upon conspicuous events, lessens the familiarity of his tale to increase its dignity, shows his favourite at a distance, decorated and magnified like the ancient actors in their tragick dress, and endeavours to hide the man that he may produce a hero.

But if it be true, which was said by a French prince, 'that no man was a hero to the servants of his chamber,' it is equally true, that every man is yet less a hero to himself. He that is most elevated above the crowd by the importance of his employ-ments, or the reputation of his genius, feels himself affected by fame or business but as they influence his domestick life. The high and low, as they have the same faculties and the same senses, have no less similitude in their pains and pleasures. The sensations are the same in all, though produced by very different occasions. The prince feels the same pain when an invader seizes a province, as the farmer when a thief drives away his cow. Men thus equal in themselves will appear equal in honest and impartial biography; and those whom fortune or nature places at the greatest distance may afford instruction to each other.

The writer of his own life has, at least, the first qualification of an historian, the knowledge of the truth; and though it may be plausibly objected that his temptations to disguise it are equal to his opportunities of knowing it, yet I cannot but think that impartiality may be expected with equal confidence from him that relates the passages of his own life, as from him that delivers the transactions of another.

Certainty of knowledge not only excludes mistake, but fortifies veracity. What we collect by conjecture, and by conjecture only, can one man judge of another's motives or sentiments, is easily modified by fancy or by desire; as objects imperfectly discerned take forms from the hope or fear of the beholder. But that which is fully known cannot be falsified but with reluctance of understanding, and alarm of conscience: of understanding, the lover of truth; of conscience, the sentinel of virtue.

He that writes the life of another is either his friend or his enemy, and wishes either to exalt his praise or aggravate his infamy: many temptations to falsehood will occur in the disguise of passions, too specious to fear much resistance. Love of virtue will animate panegyrick, and hatred of wickedness imbitter censure. The zeal of gratitude, the ardour of patriotism, fondness for an opinion, or fidelity to a party, may easily overpower the vigilance of a mind habitually well disposed, and prevail over unassisted and unfriended veracity.

But he that speaks of himself has no motive to falsehood or partiality except self-love, by which all have so often been betrayed, that all are on the watch against its artifices. He that writes an apology for a single action, to confute an accusation, to recommend himself to favour, is, indeed, always to be suspected of favouring his own cause; but he that sits down calmly and voluntarily to review his life for the admonition of posterity, or to amuse himself, and leaves this account unpublished, may be commonly presumed to tell truth, since falsehood cannot appease his own mind, and fame will not be heard beneath the tomb.

THE IDLER NO. 102
SATURDAY, MARCH 29, 1760

LITERARY
BIOGRAPHY

It very seldom happens to man that his business is his pleasure. What is done from necessity is so often to be done when against the present inclination, and so often fills the mind with anxiety, that an habitual dislike steals upon us, and we shrink involuntarily from the remembrance of our task. This is the reason why almost every one wishes to quit his employment; he does not like another state, but is disgusted with his own.

From this unwillingness to perform more than is required of that which is commonly performed with reluctance, it proceeds that few authors write their own lives. Statesmen, courtiers, ladies, generals and seamen have given to the world their own stories, and the events with which their different stations have made them acquainted. They retired to the closet as to a place of quiet and amusement, and pleased themselves with writing, because they could lay down the pen whenever they were weary. But the author, however conspicuous, or however important, either in the publick eye or in his own, leaves his life to be related by his successors, for he cannot gratify his vanity but by sacrificing his ease.

It is commonly supposed that the uniformity of a studious life affords no matter for a narration: but the truth is, that of the most studious life a great part passes without study. An author partakes of the common condition of humanity; he is born and married like another man; he has hopes and fears, expectations and disappointments, griefs and joys, and friends and enemies, like a courtier or a statesman; nor can I conceive why his affairs should not excite curiosity as much as the whisper of a drawing-room or the factions of a camp.

Nothing detains the reader's attention more powerfully than deep involutions of distress, or sudden vicissitudes of fortune; and these might be abundantly afforded by memoirs of the sons of literature. They are entangled by contracts which they know not how to fulfil, and obliged to write on subjects which they do not understand. Every publication is a new period of time, from which some increase or declension of fame is to be reckoned. The gradations of a hero's life are from battle to battle; and of an author's from book to book.

Success and miscarriage have the same effects in all conditions. The prosperous are feared, hated and flattered; and the unfortunate avoided, pitied and despised. No sooner is a book published than the writer may judge of the opinion of the world. If his acquaintance press round him in publick places, or salute him from the other side of the street; if invitations to dinner come thick upon him, and those with whom he dines keep him to supper; if the ladies turn to him when his coat is plain, and the footmen serve him with attention and alacrity; he may be sure that his work has been praised by some leader of literary fashions.

Of declining reputation the symptoms are not less easily observed. If the author enters a coffee-house, he has a box to himself; if he calls at a bookseller's, the boy turns his back; and, what is the most fatal of all prognosticks, authors will visit him in a morning, and talk to him hour after hour of the malevolence of criticks, the neglect of merit, the bad taste of the age and the candour of posterity.

All this, modified and varied by accident and custom, would form very amusing scenes of biography, and might recreate many a mind which is very little delighted with conspiracies or battles, intrigues of a court, or debates of a parliament; to this might be added all the changes of the countenance of a patron, traced from the first glow, which flattery raises in his cheek, through ardour of fondness, vehemence of promise, magnificence of praise, excuse of delay, and lamentation of inability, to the last chill look of final dismission, when the one grows weary of soliciting, and the other of hearing solicitation.

Thus copious are the materials which have been hitherto suffered to lie neglected, while the repositories of every family that has produced a soldier or a minister are ransacked, and libraries are crowded with useless folios of state-papers which will never be read, and which contribute nothing to valuable knowledge.

I hope the learned will be taught to know their own strength and their value, and, instead of devoting their lives to the honour of those who seldom thank them for their labours, resolve at last to do justice to themselves.

FURTHER READING

Anon. (Thomas Cooke), *The Life of Richard Savage who was Condemned at the Old Bailey for Murder*, London, 1727
——*Select Trials for Murder, Robberies, Rapes, Sodomy . . . in the Old Bailey*, 2 vols., London, 1734
Samuel Johnson: 'London' (poem), 1738
Denis Diderot: 'La Vie de M. Savage' (1771), in *Oeuvres Completes*, vol. IX, 1875.
Sir John Hawkins: *The Life of Samuel Johnson LL.D.*, 1787
James Boswell: *The Life of Samuel Johnson LL.D.*, (section for 'Spring 1744'), 2 vols., 1791; Oxford University Press, 1983
Charles Whitehead: *Richard Savage* (novel), 1842
J.M. Barrie: *Richard Savage*, (play), 1891
Clarence Tracy: *The Artificial Bastard: A Biography of Richard Savage*, University of Toronto Press, 1953
James L. Clifford: *Young Samuel Johnson*, Heinemann, 1955
——*The Poetical Works of Richard Savage*, edited by Clarence Tracy, Cambridge, 1962
John Wain: *Samuel Johnson*, Macmillan, 1974
Robert Folkenflik: *Samuel Johnson, Biographer*, Cornell University Press, 1978
Thomas Kaminski: *The Early Career of Samuel Johnson*, Oxford University Press, 1987
Donald Greene: 'Samuel Johnson's Life of Savage' in *The Biographer's Art*, edited by Jeffrey Meyers, Macmillan, 1989
Richard Holmes: *Dr Johnson & Mr Savage*, 1993, Harper Perennial, 2005

INDEX

Works by Richard Savage (RS) appear directly under title; works by others under author's name